# WELL READ COOKIES

## BEAUTIFUL BISCUITS INSPIRED BY GREAT LITERATURE

### LAUREN CHATER

SIMON &
SCHUSTER

London · New York · Sydney · Toronto · New Delhi

A CBS COMPANY

'FOR MY OWN PART,
IF A BOOK IS WELL
WRITTEN, I ALWAYS
FIND IT TOO SHORT.'

*CATHERINE*,
JANE AUSTEN

# WELL
# READ
# COOKIES

## BEAUTIFUL BISCUITS
## INSPIRED BY
## GREAT LITERATURE

### LAUREN CHATER

# CONTENTS

Introduction   7

*The Miniaturist* by Jessie Burton   11

*Pride and Prejudice and Zombies* by Seth Grahame-Smith   12

*The Hobbit* by J. R. R. Tolkien   15

*Alice's Adventures in Wonderland* by Lewis Carroll   16

*Sense and Sensibility* by Jane Austen   19

*Longbourn* by Jo Baker   22

*The Snow Child* by Eowyn Ivey   25

*It* by Stephen King   28

Reading Chair cookies   31

*Snow White* by the Brothers Grimm   34

*The Very Hungry Caterpillar* by Eric Carle   37

*Harry Potter and the Philosopher's Stone* by J. K. Rowling   38

*Fantastic Mr Fox* by Roald Dahl   41

*Remarkable Creatures* by Tracy Chevalier   42

*The Dinner* by Herman Koch   47

*The Little Mermaid* by Hans Christian Andersen   48

*The Secret Life of Bees* by Sue Monk Kidd   53

*The Light Between Oceans* by M. L. Stedman   54

*The Raven* by Edgar Allan Poe   58

*The Hound of the Baskervilles* by Sir Arthur Conan Doyle   61

*Dead Until Dark* by Charlaine Harris   62

*Wicked* by Gregory Maguire   65

*Sapsorrow* by the Brothers Grimm   66

*The Slap* by Christos Tsiolkas   70

*Practical Magic* by Alice Hoffman   73

*Lily and the Octopus* by Steven Rowley   76

*The Birdman's Wife* by Melissa Ashley   79

*City of Bones* by Cassandra Clare   82

*Mary Poppins* by P. L. Travers   85

*Frankenstein* by Mary Shelley   86

*Snow Flower and the Secret Fan* by Lisa See 89

*The Night Circus* by Erin Morgenstern 90

*The Great Gatsby* by F. Scott Fitzgerald 95

*Stardust* by Neil Gaiman 96

*The Lion, the Witch and the Wardrobe* by C.S. Lewis 99

*Jane Eyre* by Charlotte Brontë 100

*The Virgin Suicides* by Jeffrey Eugenides 103

*Lord of the Flies* by William Golding 106

*The North Water* by Ian McGuire 109

*The Rosie Project* by Graeme Simsion 112

*Year of Wonders* by Geraldine Brooks 115

*Foal's Bread* by Gillian Mears 118

*Anne of Green Gables* by L. M. Montgomery 121

*The German Girl* by Armando Lucas Correa 122

*Charlotte's Web* by E. B. White 125

*The Other Boleyn Girl* by Philippa Gregory 126

*The Secret Garden* by Francis Hodgson Burnett 131

*Rebecca* by Daphne du Maurier 132

*Green Eggs and Ham* by Dr. Seuss 137

*Alias Grace* by Margaret Atwood 138

*Water for Elephants* by Sara Gruen 143

*Daughter of Fortune* by Isabel Allende 144

*Chocolat* by Joanne Harris 147

*The Cinderella Murders* by Mary Higgins Clark 148

*Gone with the Wind* by Margaret Mitchell 151

*Little Women* by Louisa May Alcott 154

*The Golden Compass* by Philip Pullman 157

*Great Expectations* by Charles Dickens 158

*Interview with the Vampire* by Anne Rice 161

*Never Let Me Go* by Kazuo Ishiguro 162

Recipes, and baking and icing tips and tricks 165

Acknowledgements 174

About the author 175

# INTRODUCTION

I grew up in a house full of books.

As a child, I used books for everything – to feel better, to learn more, to escape the boredom of school holidays. Those early books shaped my understanding of different perspectives and lives lived beyond my own. I owe a great deal to all the books I've read that have touched me in some way, and this book pays homage to the best of them.

Some of my best memories are of trawling through second-hand bookshops as a child, searching for hidden gold among the shelves. I can still remember how my belly would fill with butterflies in anticipation of the moment when a book would send out an invisible call, begging to be bought, taken home and read. As an adult, I can see how the magic of reading shaped my childhood and enabled me to do what I now love, which is to write historical fiction that celebrates women's untold stories, and bake biscuits!

I started my blog *The Well Read Cookie* as a way of celebrating the books that have made me giggle, cry and sigh with pleasure. Sometimes people ask me how I come up with designs – there's no real answer, except to say that looking at art inspires me, as does the work of other cookie artists. I always sketch out my design before I start icing – royal icing in particular is notoriously quick to dry out, so speed is of the essence. I taught myself the craft by reading tips on blogs and practising (sometimes with disastrous results).

Baking and writing are not so very different. Both require liberal amounts of imagination, a dash of hope and a sprinkle of magic. I'm thrilled to be able to share with you some cookies inspired by my favourite books. I hope that in turn you'll be inspired to bake some of your own!

*Lauren*

## A NOTE FOR BAKERS

For each design in this collection I have included individual tips and ideas about how to achieve cookie nirvana, but for more comprehensive notes please go to the end of the book where I have supplied my favourite recipes and my most commonly used icing and baking techniques.

*Happy baking!*

# THE MINIATURIST

## JESSIE BURTON

Anyone who has ever lost a pet knows how dark the world can seem without them. Yes, they give us fleas and can make more mess than a pantry full of hobbits but the good always outweighs the bad. Which brings us to one of my favourite fictional pets in recent reads: Peebo the parakeet from Jessie Burton's 2017 bestselling novel set in 17th century Amsterdam.

Cheeky, chirpy and partial to a stolen nut or two, Peebo is the childhood pet of Nella Oortman, the proud owner of a whimsical cabinet of miniature wonders gifted to her by her new husband. Like Hermione Granger's cat Crookshanks and the ever plucky Old Yeller from Fred Gipson's classic, Peebo does his best to warn his mistress about what's really going on inside the Brandt household. But his chirpings are all in vain when he takes a wrong turn through an open window and flies off into the sky above Amsterdam's canals. He does make a brief return in miniature form, but that wasn't enough for me, so I decided to make these Peebo cookies in his honour.

I used a Wilton parrot cutter (the closest thing I could find to a parakeet shape) and added a pinch of cinnamon and a dab of nutmeg to give these babies a little hint of 17th century spice, but it's the green plumage and red stripes (see wet-on-wet technique below) that make these cookies uniquely 'Peebo'. Fly free, Peebo.

- To achieve a wet-on-wet look as seen on Peebo's plumage, you'll need two different bags of flooding icing ready.

- Once your cookie is flooded, quickly pipe a line of contrasting colour straight onto the wet icing.

- Drag a toothpick through the lines and allow to dry.

# PRIDE AND PREJUDICE AND ZOMBIES

## SETH GRAHAME-SMITH

This book is a scream and I'm not just talking about the bloodbath scene at the Netherfield Ball. Seth Grahame-Smith's spooky take on Jane Austen's classic is delightful and laugh-out-loud funny. Having risen from their graves to snack on the living, the great undead provide the *raison d'être* for Darcy and Elizabeth's unconventional romance.

Still considered one of the great classics to read before you die (by zombie bite or otherwise), *Pride and Prejudice* continues to enthral readers more than two centuries after initial publication. An almost mandatory inclusion in school curriculums everywhere, there's hardly an adult alive who hasn't intercepted Austen's famous comedy of manners in some way. Perhaps that's why we love to revisit it when another interpretation or parody comes out every few years. This one is an especially fiendish take which pits Elizabeth and Darcy against each other, as well as a shuffling, brain-hungry horde of the dead. *PP&Z* brings a whole new meaning to the phrase 'marry or perish'.

To make your own zombie girl cookies:

- Outline and flood the 'flesh' with white-tinted icing, leaving space for the mouth.

- Flood the mouth area and when it's dry, add in the 'bones' using a fine 1.5 mm icing tip.

- Outline and flood the dress using ivory-tinted icing, adding wet-on-wet flowers in mauve and soft pink shades. Add two dots of green for the leaves and use a toothpick to make the shape.

- Finish off by piping in the brown-tinted hair and filling in the eyes, and once the hair is dry, pipe a few flowers using an open star tip to complete.

# THE HOBBIT

## J.R.R. TOLKIEN

There's a school of thought that suggests *The Hobbit* is a better novel than *The Lord of the Rings*. I'm not saying that I necessarily support this, but think about it: there's no whining about second breakfasts, no Ents endlessly debating the merits of pacifism v. war, no love triangle – just good old-fashioned adventuring.

As a stand-alone novel, *The Hobbit* is pretty close to fantasy perfection. It's the ring of life (pun intended), a simple story about going 'there and back again'. No long-winded tangents, no false starts (well, only one), no recurring characters who pop back up à la Tom Bombadil to infuriate the reader with unwanted songs. I remember listening to the audiobook with my young son and when Tom reappeared for the third time, my son literally threw up his hands and said, 'He's back *again?*'

Plus, *The Hobbit* has a dragon. A bona fide, flame-retardant son of Glaurung who comes close to derailing the dwarves' plans to take back their treasure and reinhabit the Lonely Mountain. As is usual with dragons, Smaug's downfall is his pride. Trading riddles with our hero, he manages to expose his own weakness, a small patch of bare skin uncovered by jewels, thereby sealing his fate. It's nice to know that dragons have bad days, too. If you've ever wanted to know where Smaug's name came from, some sources suggest it's a suggestive play on words, a combination of the Slavic word for dragon – *smok* – and the primitive Germanic verb *smugen*, which literally means 'to squeeze something into a very small hole'.

When I decided to make cookies inspired by *The Hobbit*, I decided I'd have to honour Tolkien's dastardly villain and his love of treasure by sprinkling him with liberal amounts of edible 24 karat gold leaf.

Only the best for this wicked worm.

# ALICE'S ADVENTURES IN WONDERLAND

## LEWIS CARROLL

This Victorian children's classic was just *begging* to be made into iced biscuits. But what shape to choose? With such a proliferation of strange anthropomorphic creatures to choose from, I found it hard to decide on a shape that sufficiently captured the particular weirdness and whimsy of Lewis Carroll's brainchild.

The Dodo was a strong contender. Driven into extinction during the 17th century, this flightless bird was the character Carroll is said to have most strongly identified with. Then there's the Cheshire Cat, known for his wicked grin, his habit of disappearing at key moments in the journey and being a general all-round feline pain in the behind.

In the end, I couldn't go past the Dancing Lobsters. Described in great detail by the Mock Turtle (the original Emo Goth), the lobsters perform a square dance, swapping partners as they frolic in the sea foam and cleverly avoiding the notice of hungry gulls. I've dressed up my lobsters in formal dinner attire; you might like to do that, too. A lobster in a tuxedo is a charming addition to any dessert table.

I photographed these cookies on the beach in order to get the real effect of the sandy backdrop and after I was done, I let the seagulls go to town. I swear I heard the Mock Turtle cry out in horror at the waste.

For piping on the finer details, I recommend a 1.5 mm tip, which is perfect for the female lobster's necklace and the spots on her dress. You'll want to use stiff icing to ensure your details don't lose their shape. To stop the white and black icing bleeding together, I suggest icing them separately and letting one layer dry before you tackle the next.

# SENSE AND SENSIBILITY

## JANE AUSTEN

Are you Team Elinor or Team Marianne? Let me confess, dear reader, that I am an ardent member of Team Elinor. Maybe it's because I have a younger sister. As the eldest, I can't stand Marianne's whining and hand-wringing or her completely over-the-top confessions of undying love for a man she's just met. Anyone with half a brain can see that Willoughby is a cad. True love? I think not. And yet, readers continue to insist that he and Marianne should have ended up together. Common reasons given include a shared love for Shakespeare's sonnets, a preference for wildflowers (not Colonel Brandon's hothouse blooms)

and a romantic idealism that would make Childe Harold blush. Personally, I think Marianne dodged a bullet. If only she'd listened to her plainer, but considerably wiser sister. After all, it's sensible, clear-headed Elinor who finds the family a home at Barton Cottage and picks up the pieces of her sister's broken heart.

I made these miniature Teacup Barton Cottage biscuits to pay homage to Elinor's resourcefulness. They were made using a special cutter that enables you to cut each piece out and bake them separately. Then you can flood them and decorate them, allow them to dry, and glue them together with stiff piping icing.

I recommend holding the walls together while they're drying (around 10 minutes) to make sure they stick – and you can sprinkle the roof with powdered sugar (or icing sugar) to give it that English wintry look! Pop them on the rim of your teacup for an elegant Austen afternoon tea snack.

Elinor would be proud.

# LONGBOURN

## JO BAKER

They say one's home is one's castle, so if you could visit any fictional house, which would it be? Du Maurier's Manderley would surely qualify, being both home to the ghost of its former mistress and the ultimate, huge rambling English manor house. Thornfield Hall, where Rochester and Jane Eyre make google eyes at each other and fall passionately in love, would be the perfect country holiday estate if it weren't for the mad woman trapped in the attic. Personally, though, I'd rather be a fly on the wall at Longbourn where Jane Austen's Bennet family reside.

British author Jo Baker gifts us this vision with her 21st century reimagining of *Pride and Prejudice*, allowing the reader to peek below stairs at all the Bennet's dirty laundry. This is Lizzie and Darcy as you've never seen them before: haughty, hairy *breeders* who are just as trapped within the roles society demands of them as their inferiors. In fact, it's the servants who have more freedom in *Longbourn* than those with millionaire incomes (adjusting Mr Darcy's 10,000 pounds to allow for inflation). Who else but a servant could laugh about Mr Collins's ridiculous manoeuvres to obtain the object of his choice without fear of succumbing to the same matrimonial fate? *Longbourn* reminds us that there's always a silver lining, no matter how poor you are.

When I put these Lizzie and Darcy cookies together, I wanted to give them a flocked floral look so I flooded them with ivory icing, then, using a 1.5 mm fine tip, I hand-piped scrolls and flourishes on top. You can get this look by studying old wallpapers and copying the patterns onto your biscuits! It's a good idea to practice on a bit of wax paper first.

# THE SNOW CHILD

## EOWYN IVEY

When I was a kid, I loved fairytales. Disney was my go-to guide to the magical, adventure-laden world of talking animals and enchanted inanimate objects (don't judge me, it was the eighties). I wanted to be a princess in a swirling gown who battled the odds and got her happy ending and her prince.

And then when I was seven, I read a young reader's edition of Eastern European folk stories, which included *The Snow Child*. An old Slavic fairytale, it's the story of an old peasant couple who are deeply unhappy since they can't have kids. Their solution? Build one out of snow, naturally. Lo and behold, the snow child comes to life and they give her a name – Snyergurka – and raise her as their child. One day Snyergurka is playing with her friends and she jumps over a fire and *poof*! She's a puddle. The old couple are heartbroken. That's it. No ballgowns, no prince, and definitely no happy ending.

When I heard Eowyn Ivey had adapted the folk story and set it in the Alaskan wilderness, I inhaled it immediately and then had to make cookies to honour the day I read and loved the original as a child, which was also the day I learned fairytales were actually dark and twisted and intended to act as warnings.

I chose to make snowflakes to reflect the icy-cold landscape evoked in the novel. You can make these with a dark gingerbread base, too (the recipe is on page 166) – it really sets off the lemony icing to perfection. Start by outlining and flooding the snowflakes, then pipe your details on top with a 1.5 mm tip. I like to pop little coloured cachous on while the icing is still wet, but you could always sprinkle sugar instead to achieve a sparkling, winter-frosted look.

# IT

## STEPHEN KING

Stephen King has a lot to answer for.

In the 1980s, he single-handedly traumatised a generation of children who can no longer stand the sight of drains or clowns. King's terrifying character, a demented child-eating clown called Pennywise, is a modern-day version of the troll hiding under the bridge, made famous by that classic kids' folktale *The Three Billy Goats Gruff*. The kids in the town of Derry, Maine, all see Pennywise differently. That's what makes him so frightening. He's every circus clown you've ever laughed at, every Ronald McDonald who handed you a burger on McHappy Day.

There's just something about clowns that gets under the skin and creeps into nightmares. King knows this, and like any great storyteller, he taps into our collective consciousness and serves up one of the horror genre's most disturbing and memorable villains of all time.

I made these Pennywise balloon cookies to celebrate the recent movie adaptation, but they're good for late-night horror marathons and Halloween, too. I used a balloon cutter to give them their shape, flooded them with yellow icing and decorated the top layer with bloody handprints using a 1.5 mm fine tip. I also added baker's twine as balloon string once the biscuits were dry. Use a bit of stiff icing to glue the string onto the back of the cookie. Go ahead and give them a whirl!

As the ghost of poor Georgie Denbrough tells his brother Bill, you'll float as well!

(Severed arm not guaranteed.)

# READING CHAIR COOKIES

Bookworms. Bibliophiles. Book-lovers. Call us what you like, we'll just keep on reading. The term 'bibliophile' first appeared in the English language in 1824 and was used to describe 'one who loves to read, collect and admire' books, sometimes to the detriment of all else. Book tragics like me – and most likely you – often prefer to live in fictitious worlds and resent being dragged back to reality to undertake mundane tasks such as putting the bins out and feeding the cat.

Some of history's most famous bibliophiles include author Ernest Hemingway (9,000 books), food writer and television personality Nigella Lawson (6,000 books) and master escape artist Harry Houdini (4,000 books), who is believed to have once possessed the largest collection of magic books in the world. Then there's Thomas Jefferson, the third President of the United States, who once stated, 'I cannot live without books.' In 1814, Jefferson sold his entire personal library to pay off substantial debts. However, after only paying off a portion, he began frantically collecting volumes again. Once a bibliophile, always a bibliophile.

These reading chair cookies, inspired by the perfect place to curl up and dive into another world, were decorated using a stencil to achieve the consistent flocked look of the icing. Stencils are great for small batches of cookies but not particularly good for a hundred or more, as they require cleaning in between each use in order to get a nice, crisp outline. Here's how to use them:

- Line up the stencil over the cookie.

- Using a spatula, spread a layer of icing across the stencil, ensuring every gap is covered. Try to keep the layer thin – too much icing will result in the pattern losing its shape.

- Pull the stencil carefully away and admire your work!

# SNOW WHITE

## THE BROTHERS GRIMM

The Snow White fairytale has always courted controversy. Originally written in 1812 by the Grimm brothers Jacob and Wilhelm, this infamous story features more fairytale tropes than you can poke a stick at. Magic mirror? Check. Poison apple? Gotcha. Evil Queen who demands her stepdaughter's bloody eviscerated heart as proof of her demise? You bet. And of course there are the dwarves (who, in the original version, came home to find that Snow had trashed their place like a rock star on her first road trip).

After apologising, little Snow agrees to keep house for the men. That's one girl living with *seven men*. My grandmother would have a conniption! Among the many remakes and retellings over the years, Disney's version of the tale is perhaps the most recognisable. As the first fairytale chosen by Walt Disney productions to be made into a full-length animated feature, there was always going to be pressure on *Snow White and the Seven Dwarves* to deliver the goods, but the movie was an all-out box-office success. I bet the studio was glad they reduced the number of dwarves down from Walt Disney's original suggestion of FIFTY to seven.

Much to my disappointment, one of the other things Walt changed was the scene where Snow's stepmother, disguised as a peddler, gives Snow a magical corset designed to squeeze her to death. Luckily, the dwarves come home just in the nick of time and cut her loose. Disney decided he didn't want Snow White to appear too 'sexualised' (because, you know, the references to Betty Boop were a complete coincidence) so he went with the poisoned apple instead.

I made these corset cookies to restore the balance. They also make great favours for a hen's night.

# THE VERY HUNGRY CATERPILLAR

## ERIC CARLE

Why are children so obsessed with books about food? From *Charlie and the Chocolate Factory* to *Possum Magic*, food and literature continues to be an utterly magical combination. What is it that makes us go gaga for Suessian green eggs and ham and dreamy Sendak-style aeroplane doughnuts? Psychologists suggest food is associated with memory, so perhaps when parents read to children from picture books which feature fantastical feasts and pleasant picnics, a love of food is absorbed along with the language.

Nowhere is this combination of edibles and idioms more apparent than in Eric Carle's classic tale of gluttony and greed, *The Very Hungry Caterpillar*. Brimful of fruit, condiments and sweets, it's the ultimate guide to a week's worth of overeating, but it's also a lesson in growth and transformation.

The compulsion of the caterpillar to consume everything in sight is an instantly recognisable childish trait. The mere whiff of a pickle takes me straight back to my school days, and whenever the words 'chocolate' and 'cake' are mentioned together, I find myself reaching for the fridge – because, as everyone knows, the perfect accompaniment to a Matilda-style Bruce Bogtrotter chocolate cake (thank you Roald Dahl) is a slice of Swiss cheese.

When I was making these hungry caterpillar cookies, my children offered very helpfully to cut the holes out of the 'fruits' instead of what they usually do, which is squirt the icing straight into their mouths. I recommend using the bottom of an icing tip to get a good-sized hole and piping an outline around the hole first before you flood so that the icing doesn't drip down inside. You'll need a 1.5 mm tip for the caterpillar's details.

# HARRY POTTER AND THE PHILOSOPHER'S STONE

## J.K. ROWLING

Ever since the release of J. K. Rowling's first Harry Potter book, publishers all over the world have been trying to pinpoint its success. What is the secret ingredient in that first book that keeps readers of all ages coming back for more? Well, I'm here to tell you, right now, as well as the delicious idea that kids can use magic to roam outside the control of adults, doing whatever the hell they like (illicit broomstick flying, third-floor corridor trespass), for me it's the *flying keys*.

Magically enchanted, the winged keys are part of Harry's final trial before he faces off against his arch nemesis, the evil (and, at this time, incorporeal) Voldemort. For me, these keys capture the charm and whimsy that lies at the heart of Rowling's story. I had the cookie cutter for these winged keys custom-made by a friend who uses a 3D printer to create whatever fantastical cookies I come up with. You can always cut them out by hand, but it can be a tiring process if you've got more than, say, a dozen to make in one go. If you do decide to hand cut them, use the following tips to ensure success:

- Draw your design in pen on a sheet of semi-stiff cardboard and then cut it out with scissors. Paper is okay, too, but the butter tends to bleed and by the time you've reached your last cookie, the paper may be so flimsy it's in danger of ripping.

- Place the cardboard on your rolled-out dough and using a scalpel or sharp blade (non-serrated, if possible), cut carefully around the shape.

- Rub your thumb along bumps or jagged edges to smooth the dough, then arrange as usual on a flat tray and bake as normal.

# FANTASTIC MR FOX

## ROALD DAHL

Boggis, Bunce and Bean ... the names of these horrible villains will forever remain part of my childhood. I adore Roald Dahl for his charm, his daring and the darkness that is present in each and every one of his tales.

As a child (and I'm not ashamed to admit this) I was a glutton. Every time my dad read *Fantastic Mr Fox* out loud to us as kids, I would fall asleep to visions of delicious cooked chicken, jellied doughnuts and glistening jugs of Bean's apple cider ale, which I imagined to be something like fizzy apple juice. I have no doubt Dahl intended to make *Fantastic Mr Fox* so appealing in the food stakes. He was an incredibly perceptive writer and nowhere is his capacity to captivate the childish obsession with food more evident than in the iconic *Charlie and the Chocolate Factory*. Hunger is actually one of the driving forces in *Fantastic Mr Fox* – without food, Mr Fox's family will starve, so the stakes are raised and the scene set for a showdown with his band of human nemeses, the three Bs.

Fox cookies are particularly joyful to make and they don't have to be difficult. In fact, the simpler the better. I tinted Mr Fox's coat with three toothpicks of electric orange colouring. Any more than that and you run the risk of giving him a bright red coat rather than a more distinguished russet.

If you aren't feeling confident about piping the facial details without a guide, use an edible marker to draw on the lines where his white cheeks will be. Pipe and flood his white paws last and enjoy with a tall glass of cider siphoned directly from Bean's storehouse.

# REMARKABLE CREATURES

## TRACY CHEVALIER

Tracy Chevalier is perhaps best known for her reimagining of one of the world's most recognised paintings, Vermeer's *Girl with a Pearl Earring*, but she is also the author of a wonderful historical novel based on the life of Mary Anning. Eccentric fossil-hunter and original Independent Woman, Anning was struck by lightning as a baby but survived to make her first big fossil discovery – a complete specimen of an ichthyosaur – at the age of 12.

In a time when men ruled the scientific world, Anning's discovery prompted many controversial ideas about God and the natural world. Her 'curies' (little fossils

shaped like coiled snakes) were fashionably collected by visitors to Lyme Regis, where she lived. I enjoyed reading Chevalier's retelling of Anning's life so much I had to honour her contribution by making these quaint iced ammonites.

Try these tips and this variation on the vanilla dough recipe to achieve a dark chocolate brownie base, which will give your fossil cookies that authentic 'just-dug-up-from-the-ground' look:

- Substitute ½ cup flour for ½ cup cocoa powder (dark is best but at a pinch, light will do).

- Substitute white sugar for dark brown sugar.

- When rolling out your dough, sift some cocoa powder instead of plain flour onto your mat to prevent stickiness.

- Any round or oval cutter will do for the ammonite shape. Flood your cookie first with ivory-tinted icing, allow to dry, then pipe your details on top using a 2 mm tip.

# THE DINNER

## HERMAN KOCH

Who hasn't been to a family get-together and found themselves wishing that everyone would simultaneously come down with food poisoning just so you could all go home? Herman Koch's *The Dinner* parodies all those enforced labour-camp-with-your-family meals in the best way and serves up a dessert of stone-cold transgenerational revenge. Set in a gourmet restaurant in The Hague, this novel is so cleverly sectioned into Appetisers, Mains and Desserts that I had trouble deciding what cookie would be the best to pay homage to this delightfully nasty bit of wordplay.

The twist in the novel is that although the food sounds delicious, it's all poisoned with spiteful memories, and the main character Paul can't even taste it because his medication has dulled the flavours.

In the end I went with a cookie lobster, brightened by a side garnish of iced lettuce and lemon. I advise icing the lobster shell in sections, to give it some texture. Don't forget to let them dry in between or you'll end up with a red hot mess similar to the one Paul's made of his life.

To make the lemon wedge, have both your lemon yellow and bright white-tinted icing on hand, ready for the wet-on-wet technique. After flooding your cookie with white icing, draw a small curve of yellow for the lemon rind and then drag a toothpick through the colour to create the lemon segments.

Please note that serving these cookies to your family will not give them food poisoning!

# THE LITTLE MERMAID

## HANS CHRISTIAN ANDERSEN

Long before Disney introduced rebellious red-haired adolescent mermaid Ariel to the world, Danish writer Hans Christian Andersen wrote the original cautionary tale about love and sacrifice. Published in 1837, it follows the now-familiar story of fish-girl meets boy, but with a few notable exceptions.

The ending, for example, is much darker, as the deal Andersen's mermaid makes with the sea witch means every step she takes on land is like 'a thousand razor blades' cutting into the soles of her feet.

Ouch! Although her fishy sisters try to rescue her, Little M refuses to kill her prince to save her own life and instead throws herself into the water to become sea foam. There's also no singing crabs and no fabulous drag queen-inspired sea witch.

But what Andersen's fairytale does give us inspiration for is a beautiful muted colour cookie palette. Lots of cookies use very bright food-dye colours to attract attention, but with something like *The Little Mermaid*, I wanted to make the tones a little more natural.

Here's a tip: if you mix a tiny toothpick-sized amount of colour into your tinted icing, the final colour will be much less garish. For the mermaid's tail, I used a tiny spot of ivory colouring mixed with teal-tinted icing. Mix the colour well so it all blends in – you should end up with a duck-egg blue.

Before you pipe and flood the tails, make up some dark royal-blue tinted icing so you can create the wet-on-wet effect. Pipe lines across the tail, then drag a toothpick through the icing to create the rippling water effect. Finish off the mermaid's body using flesh-tone tinted icing, and colour her hair in any shade you choose. I like to pop a few cachous or edible pearls on her hair while it's still drying.

Every mermaid worth her salt deserves pearls in her hair.

# THE SECRET LIFE OF BEES

## SUE MONK KIDD

Here are some things you probably didn't know about bees:

- A single worker bee makes only 1/12 of a teaspoon of honey in a season.

- A bee might visit over 2,000 flowers in a single day.

- If a hive loses their queen, they can make an 'emergency' one by feeding her replacement royal jelly exclusively, instead of her usual diet of bee-toast and honey.

Bees are absolutely amazing creatures. They are also the inspiration behind one of my favourite novels, *The Secret Life of Bees*. This coming-of-age tale has so much going for it – gorgeous writing, a sleepy Southern setting and a teenage protagonist you just can't help falling in love with.

First published in 2001, *The Secret Life of Bees* also managed to elevate bee knowledge and folklore into mainstream fiction. Apart from the beautiful research woven through the story, it's a tender portrayal of a girl on the cusp of womanhood who follows the clues left behind by her mother and, in the process, finds her family and herself.

With their gold-striped bodies and edible lustre-dusted wings, these cookies were a joy to make! Try this variation to add some honey and spice to your biscuit base:

- Substitute 1/2 cup sugar for 1/2 cup honey.

- Add 1/2 teaspoon of cinnamon.

- If you're feeling very adventurous, you could add in 1 teaspoon of cracked black pepper. The resulting biscuit will be a little spicy but all good things are, right?

# THE LIGHT BETWEEN OCEANS

## M.L. STEDMAN

Ever since I was a little kid, I've wanted to live in a lighthouse. They were built for children (or introverts), really. Those circular stairs! That big bright light that signals protection and safety! Those windows that look like they're built to shoot arrows out of!

But when you grow up, you realise lighthouses aren't all they're cracked up to be. There's the isolation and the loneliness, for starters. The emergency wake-up calls of ships signalling distress. And there's the cold. I once visited a lighthouse in the

Bass Strait, which separates Tasmania from mainland Australia, and I don't think I've ever been warm since.

No, lighthouses are *definitely* not all they're cracked up to be. They also harbour secrets; hushed-up maritime disasters, small-town affairs, family betrayals. What's that saying? At the edge of the ocean, nobody can hear you scream? M. L. Stedman successfully tapped into this with her brilliant, evocative novel *The Light Between Oceans*. Featuring a lighthouse, a child of mysterious parentage and a couple who are faced with a moral choice, Stedman's book had all the ingredients for a heart-wrenching story and, even more excitingly, cookies.

My lighthouse cookies were iced using alternating bright white and red-tinted icing. Let one section dry before you move onto the next so the colours don't bleed. I used a 1.5 mm tip to pipe in the light – that symbol of human connectedness outshining the dark – and while it was still drying, I scattered some edible glitter on top to give it an extra bit of real-life sparkle.

# THE RAVEN

## EDGAR ALLAN POE

Considered by many to be Edgar Allan Poe's most recognised work, *The Raven*, a narrative poem about a man who goes mad pining for his dead wife, has terrifed and delighted readers since its publication in 1845. The idea of the common raven as harbinger of death and madness is popular in both fiction and folklore. Who hasn't heard the term 'a murder of crows'? Alternative collective groupings are a 'conspiracy of crows' and an 'unkindness of crows'. Found in both Europe and America, perhaps some of the best known crows are the ones raised at the Tower of London, where they are tended by a local Ravenmaster. Now almost as famous as the Crown Jewels, the crows are a popular attraction, as is the mythology which suggests that if the crows ever disappear from the Tower, the monarchy will fall. If that's not an endorsement to treat crows kindly, I don't know what is.

Although *The Raven* did make Poe famous, it sadly didn't make him rich. Quite fitting for a poem about a bird from hell. The poem itself, which describes a man's descent into madness after the death of his lover (the 'lost Lenore') is fantastically dark and creepy and so much fun to read aloud on a cold winter's night in front of a fire. It also makes an excellent literary drinking game. I guarantee that if you take a shot every time that damn bird quotes 'Nevermore', you'll be sozzled quicker than a character from a Tennessee Williams play (not that I endorse that sort of thing).

For these raven cookies, I used pure black-tinted royal icing with just a hint of midnight blue (one toothpick should suffice) to give the colour depth. I must warn you that if you eat these cookies, your mouth, your tongue and quite possibly your soul will turn black as pitch. You have been warned.

# THE HOUND OF THE BASKERVILLES

## SIR ARTHUR CONAN DOYLE

Long before Stephen King turned the pet dog into a source of slobbering terror with his novel *Cujo*, Arthur Conan Doyle delivered the creepy canine goods in *The Hound of the Baskervilles* in 1902.

Conan Doyle apparently based the hound on a number of real legends such as the fearsome supernaturnal hound of Yeth who stalked the streets of Devon, an English county. Black dogs in particular were believed by superstitious Brits to be associated with death and the Devil, although it turns out in Conan Doyle's tale that the creature is a mixed-breed Mastiff and Bloodhound, painted with phospheresence to emit a ghostly glow. I failed to find any evidence of how the breeders of these particular dogs responded to Conan Doyle's maligning of their much-loved puppers, but in any case, the real murderer at the heart of the story is not the crazy canine but a psychopathic naturalist with a penchant for hunting moths.

Butterfly cookies are extremely popular for birthdays and Easter celebrations but if your book club has chosen *The Hound of the Baskervilles* for its next read, might I suggest these alternative Lepidoptera for a fun twist on the original?

I used a traditional butterfly cutter to make these moth cookies and copied a photograph of a real moth to get the right look. A few tips:

- Ice the fore and hindwings in sections, allowing them to dry in between.

- Using a 1.5 mm icing tip, draw dark circles straight into your still-wet ivory-tinted icing (this is the wet-on-wet technique). This ensures the end result is 'flat', just like a real moth's wing.

- After drying, dust the moth cookies with brown lustre dust.

# DEAD UNTIL DARK

## CHARLAINE HARRIS

Y'all might remember that time back in 2001 when a psychic barmaid and a SNAV (that's sensitive new-age vampire) hit the urban fantasy scene and completely challenged everything we thought we knew about the world of the undead. Sultry Bon Temps, Louisiana, makes the perfect setting for Charlaine Harris's first book in the Sookie Stackhouse Mystery series. With a cast of characters as colourful as a bag of Skittles, the only thing more appealing than sex with Eric the Vampire is the bottled blood ('True Blood'), synthetically manufactured in Japan, which allows the walking undead to mingle with the humans.

I love the whole aesthetic of this novel – the gator-infested swamps, the 'fang-bangers' (vampire-obsessed groupies), the whole Southern vibe of Merlotte's Bar and Grill. This book was almost the antithesis of *Twilight* – the vampires in Renard Parish are nasty fiends and they sure as heck don't sparkle. I think some True Blood style cookies would make the perfect Melotte's dessert after a cheeseburger and fries (and a bit of the red stuff).

A beer bottle cutter is your best choice for achieving this look. I flooded the cookies with reddish-brown tinted icing, then waited until they were dry before adding the drops of condensation with a 1.5 mm icing tip. I piped the bottle cap on freestyle and added the labels last.

If you want to give your cookies a more authentic Louisiana flavour, add three drops of pure lime essence to the icing while it's mixing.

Better than Adele's Key Lime Pie!

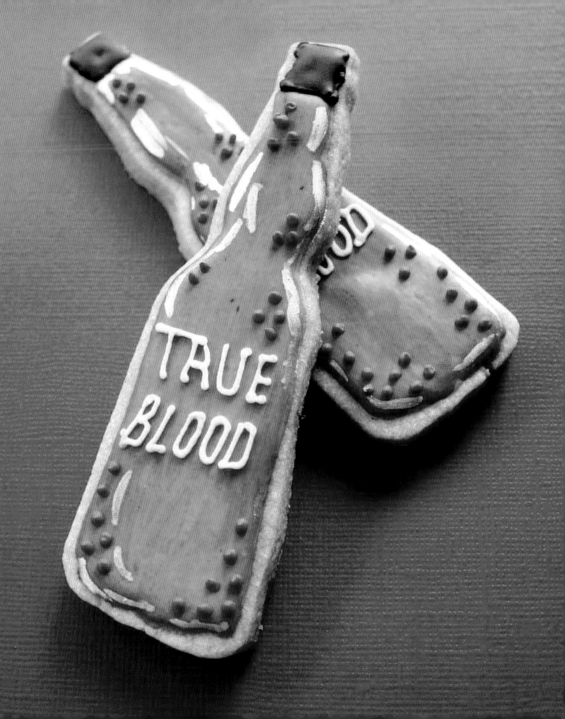

# WICKED

## GREGORY MAGUIRE

What does it mean to be wicked? Gregory Maguire gives us a clue in this diabolically twisted vision of Frank L. Baum's *The Wizard of Oz*. Green-skinned book nerd Elphaba Thropp (eventually known by her infamous sobriquet The Wicked Witch of the West) is a completely charming heroine and you can't help but fall under her spell as she navigates the dangerous world of boys, school gossip and black magic. Elphaba's viridian hue is the result of a mysterious elixir given to her mother by a travelling salesman, but what hooked me into the story was when baby Elphie said her first word: 'Horrors!' The book only gets better from there, expanding the original Oz story to include a political allegory about courage and resistance and an exploration of the complexities of female friendship.

Many elements of Baum's novel were inspired by his childhood. He had a recurring nightmare about a scarecrow pursuing him across a field, and The Wizard was informed by John D. Rockefeller, an oil magnate whose success in business was based on how cheaply he could acquire his competitor's companies. At one point in the novel, the Wizard is described as 'tyrranical and hairless'; Rockefeller suffered a medical condition that caused him to lose every strand on his head.

Just like Baum's story, at the heart of *Wicked* is one girl's search for home – only in this case, the plucky heroine isn't the one with the red shoes but the smart girl with the big hat.

Elphaba cookies make fantastic gifts for Halloween for any literary-obsessed friends. I used a custom cutter for her hat and face, but you could cut these shapes by hand. Pipe and flood the hat first, then allow to dry before adding the face. I used a shade of electric green for Elphaba's skin and added just the smallest amount to my white icing. Add the lip details with a fine 1.5 mm tip.

# SAPSORROW

## THE BROTHERS GRIMM

Long before pink pussy hats and activated almonds were a thing, the world faced a very different sort of controversy when the anti-fur movement had its first big breakthrough and protestors infiltrated Fashion Week in New York to support animal rights by throwing buckets of paint at the fur-clad models. Thankfully, their protests worked and most designers now use faux fur, which is fabulous and cruelty-free! Clearly ahead of its time, this 19th century Grimm Brothers fairytale sidesteps that whole delicate issue of ethical production by having forest animals 'donate' a tiny little bit of their fur to the heroine, who stitches them into a cloak and enabling her to escape marriage with her father.

This folktale has something for everyone, not just animal rights supporters. It's about finding the courage to be yourself, trusting the universe to come up with the princely goods and always being kind to your friends, animal and human alike. As a bonus, we get some mighty fine dresses to drool over. When the princess in the story is left bereft by her mother's death, she's surprised to learn that her father promised he would only marry someone who was as beautiful as his dying wife – and even more horrified to find out that Daddy Dearest has designed this to satisfy his own lustful urges. Yes, you heard that right; he plans to marry his own daughter. Cornered by her lecherous father, Sapsorrow tries to delay the marriage by asking Dad to have three dresses made for her – one as white as starlight, one as silver as the moon and one as gold as the sun.

Unfortunately, Dad also puts the hard word on the palace seamstress so the dresses are made lickety-split. That's when Sapsorrow has to ask her animal friends for help and of course, because she's such a good, kind girl, they bail her out with a patchwork cloak made from fur. She escapes and goes on to catch the eye of a neighbouring prince who marries her.

The beautiful dresses in Sapsorrow were the inspiration behind these cookies. I recommend painting on a little edible gold dust mixed with a little rose spirit after the scrolls and flourishes have dried.

There are many dress-shaped cookie cutters around, but I'm particularly partial to my copper cutters. The difference between copper and aluminium is negligible, but copper cutters do last longer if you look after them. They also make beautiful Christmas decorations. Use a bit of baker's twine and hang them up on your tree for an alternative to traditional tree swag (just don't forget to wipe off the crusty dough bits first!).

# THE SLAP

## CHRISTOS TSIOLKAS

Cherubs, nippers, rugrats, toddlers, brats. Call them what you will, children are an endlessly fascinating source of material to authors everywhere. Everyone has a different opinion on how to discipline them, feed them and get them to sleep, but there's one thing we can all agree on: kids are hard work. Full of sharp observations, *The Slap* is a biting commentary on middle-class power structures, and Tsiolkas focuses particularly on how we raise our children and where our responsibility lies.

The titular slap takes place in a typical Australian backyard (more commonly recognised as the setting for impromptu cricket games and bad sunburn) and most of the characters are pretty self-absorbed and unlikeable, but Tsiolkas delights in holding a mirror up to show us who we are – the good, the bad and the extremely nasty – and this is where its brilliance lies. The main characters in *The Slap* are not, of course, the worst fictional parents encountered in literature. A race to the bottom of fiction's most horrible parents and guardians must surely include:

- The Dursleys

- Fagin

- Mr and Mrs Wormwood

If your bookclub is one of those groups that likes to get drunk and debate the choices of a book's characters, then I urge you to try *The Slap* and, while you're at it, whip up some of these barbecue cookies for good measure.

In order to make a Weber Q (a famous Australian barbecue brand), you'll need to find a barbecue cookie cutter or hand cut one yourself. Pipe and flood with red-tinted icing and allow to dry before adding the details in silver-tinted icing in a bag fitted with a 1.5 mm fine tip.

# PRACTICAL MAGIC

## ALICE HOFFMAN

Popular culture enjoyed something of a pagan revival in the 1990s and Alice Hoffman's bewitching novel about small towns, spells and sisterhood ignited the zeitgeist to fever pitch. For a while there, it was considered very bad taste to leave the house without first misting yourself from head to toe with Impulse spray and adding some 'exotic' butterfly clips to your hair.

The girls I went to school with sat on the lawn and read *Practical Magic* and Fiona Horne's *The Naked Witch* aloud to each other before debating the merits of which spell to use to charm their potential love interests after class. I have no idea if the charms worked – I suspect not – but the point is, there was something about the shared camaraderie of the witchy sisterhood that made adolescence seem so much more bearable. If you had a similar experience (I won't tell), then you need to relive your youth by baking up a batch of these lavender-infused *Prac Mag* cookies, inspired by Alice Hoffman's iconic and best-loved novel.

Culinary lavender is harvested from specially grown plants and can be found in most food supply or organic ingredient companies. It's super easy to use – just add 2 tablespoons (or more if you want a stronger flavour) in at the dough-making stage and bake as per usual. You may find that the lavender flakes off a little, creating a slightly pitted surface in your cookie, but any holes are easily filled with royal icing.

# LILY AND THE OCTOPUS

## STEVEN ROWLEY

Who doesn't love a dog in a book? From Lassie to Toto and everything in between, readers can't get enough of literary pooches. Fictional dogs are the best for the simple reason that everyone gets to enjoy their antics without having to clean their dirty paw prints off the white lounge.

Steven Rowley's first novel follows the adventures of the adorably well-groomed Lily the Daschund. Like *Marley and Me* by Josh Grogan and the equally wonderful *The Traveling Cat Chronicles* by Hiro Arikawa, *Lily and the Octopus* doesn't just explore the secret life of pets but how those animals enrich their owners' lives with humour and joy. With such short life spans (compared to humans, anyway), it's inevitable that pets will age and pass on before us, but the inevitability of the grief to come doesn't put us off adopting them. On the contrary, it's a privilege to own a pet, and Lily, a high-spirited Daschund, might be battling her own 'octopus', but dammit, she's going to have one last big adventure and help her owner Ted get his life on track. Pass the tissues, please!

Curious, brave and charming, Daschunds are *everybody's* cup of tea and Lily makes friends wherever she goes. Just do NOT call her a weiner! Of course, now that the world has fallen in love with *Lily and the Octopus*, there's a rash of mini-dashes running about everywhere. There's nothing like life imitating book.

These Lily cookies were made from a custom-cutter but Daschunds are so popular it wouldn't be hard to find a ready-made one. I gave my Lily a misting of edible shimmer spray just because I felt she could use more sparkle. I used an airbrush gun, but you can also buy cans of edible shimmer spray if you don't want the hassle.

# THE BIRDMAN'S WIFE

**MELISSA ASHLEY**

Books about taxidermy occupy a very unusual spot in literature. After reading Melissa Ashley's debut novel, a vibrant reimagining of the life of 19th century artist Elizabeth Gould, I was keen to explore the dark side and find out if anyone else had been brave enough to write about this macabre topic.

My research led me to quite a few places (including the hilarious *Crap Taxidermy* – I recommend), but none of the books I read were as good as *The Birdman's Wife*. Somehow, Ashley manages to get right under the skin (oops!) of her characters and inject the perfect amount of tension into the story of this little-known Australian artist. Bad puns aside, the book was an eye-opener into the way 19th century English migrants responded to the Australian landscape by attempting to study and tame its elusive fauna and wildlife – and thereby understand themselves. And thankfully, attitudes about the preservation of wildlife are changing as society develops a more respectful response.

I used a copper cookie cutter to make these delicate hummingbirds – which were painted by Elizabeth Gould and referenced in the book – and edible paint to create the watercolour effect of the feathers.

A few tips about using edible paint:

- It's best to apply edible paint sparingly using a good brush. If you use too much in one go, it creates pockmarks or holes in the icing which is not the look you're going for.

- I recommend a nice watercolour sable-hair brush if you can get it. Your cookies are works of art, like Elizabeth Gould's, so you want the best quality brush you can afford!

# CITY OF BONES

## CASSANDRA CLARE

The YA literary scene (that's 'Young Adult' to the uninitiated) has been growing in popularity for many years now, helped along by a healthy dose of sparkly vampire hunkiness (*Twilight*) and starving teenage heroine-ism (*The Hunger Games*). Cassandra Clare's *City of Bones* is the first in her series of books which explores the dark underworld of demons and the adolescent Shadowhunters whose job it is to find and destroy them. What a romp through teen-town this book is!

It's got everything, from magical Tarot cards to a gay warlock who styles himself the High Warlock of Brooklyn. The magic of the story is not just in how Clare puts surprising twists on familiar scenarios, but the actual bad-assery of the weapons and charms the Shadowhunters use. For example, in order to protect themselves from monsters, the teenagers ink their skin with a 'stele', a kind of portable tattoo gun. As someone who recently got their third tattoo (sorry Mum!), I can only imagine the torture of carving protective symbols into your skin before every single battle. Ouch! It does ratchet up the sexy slash cool factor, though…

These stele cookies were inspired by the Shadowhunters' instrument of pain – I mean, protection. Create your own by using a plaque cookie cutter and piping swords with silver scrolls across the surface when the base is fully dry. I added a few hints of edible silver, to give it that Shadowhunter edge.

# MARY POPPINS

## P.L. TRAVERS

There have been many moments since I had children when I have dearly wished for a nanny, the old-fashioned kind who breezes in with a bag of toys in one hand and a hip-flask in the other. But this is the cruel joke the universe plays on us when we grow up: amazing magical nannies like Mary Poppins do not exist in real life. Perhaps that's why I enjoy reading this book to my kids so much; I can still pretend there's a chance she might show up.

Prim and proper, Poppins arrives at Cherry Tree Lane with her carpet bag, blown in by a very gusty East Wind under sail of her magical umbrella, which I've always thought was the most useful of her accessories. When the wind changes, she just opens it up, catches the next breeze and pops off to visit new families who need her most. What a life!

These Edwardian Mary Poppins umbrellas are so fun to make. Be careful when you're pushing the dough out of the handle part of the cutter as it can be fragile. Here are a few other tips on how to ensure your cookies are perfectly baked every time:

- Dust your cutter in flour before each use.

- If the dough gets stuck, use a toothpick to gently wriggle it free.

- If you do get some breakage (and you can't be bothered cutting again), see if you can gently reattach the broken part then quickly freeze the tray for at least 20 minutes. The dough should bond back together.

# FRANKENSTEIN; OR, THE MODERN PROMETHEUS

## MARY SHELLEY

Forever doomed to wander the icy wastelands of Antarctica (and to have his name mistakenly confused with that of his creator), the monster at the heart of Shelley's novel has become a cult icon in his own right. Stitched together from the gross body parts of various unclaimed victims, Frankenstein both thrills and horrifies (much like an episode of *Keeping Up With the Kardashians*), and the monster's namesake has been used to describe everything from apple soda to a product or a service that has been hastily cobbled together.

The genesis of the Frankenstein story is almost as fabulous as the book, by the way; Mary Shelley claimed to have dreamed it up in response to a challenge by her friends that she couldn't deliver a really good horror story. Holed up in a chateau in the Swiss Alps with her lover Percy Shelley, the writer Lord Byron and their friend John Polidori, Shelley constructed the story from a dream she'd had, combined with a passing interest in galvanism, the reanimation of a corpse via electrical current. After starting what she assumed would be a short ghost story, she soon realised she was writing a novel. Challenge accepted – and horror delivered. Shelley's tale was so good, in fact, that it went on to be published and has never been out of print.

These candlestick cookies make great snacks to accompany a reading of *Frankenstein*. Without electricity, in the 18th century (when *Frankenstein* is set), people had to rely on candlelight and keeping fires going all year round in order to see after dark. Frankenstein's monster knows this and uses the darkness to move around undetected and carry out his revenge on poor Victor's bride.

I divided these cookies into three sections; the black base, the white candle and the wet-on-wet flame. Allow each section to dry individually before moving on so the colours don't bleed.

# SNOW FLOWER AND THE SECRET FAN

## LISA SEE

I have such fond memories of writing coded messages to my best friend when I was child, but I never realised that secret languages existed until I read Lisa See's brilliant novel about female friendship, set in 19th century China. Nushu, a secret phonetic women's-only language, is used by the story's main characters, two 'sworn sisters', to communicate their thoughts and feelings and sentiments that were dangerous to express in the claustrophobic, male-dominated culture of 1800s China. The women inscribe their thoughts on the delicate folds of a paper fan which they pass to each other. This is a much more sophisticated system than the one my bestie and I used, where we wrote in lemon ink on ripped-out pieces of foolscap from our schoolbooks then burnt them under the grill to make the words appear. I can't tell you how many times we set off the fire alarm. Our confessions were the stuff of bored kids, though; the stories that Lily and Snow Flower tell each other are marred by pain, both psychological (marriage, the death of children) and physical (foot-binding and the horror of the Taiping Rebellion, where millions were killed for defying the Emperor). Through a secret language, the women sustain each other, which makes for a very beautiful and moving exploration of the value of female friendship.

To make these beautiful fans, you can use a pizza cookie cutter like I did, or you can buy a specific fan shape (I've seen plenty around).

- Pipe the edges in brown-tinted icing, then flood the middle section with white icing.

- Create the 'folds' of the fan by piping thin lines with grey-tinted icing.

- After allowing the middle section to dry, fill a piping bag with stiff pink-tinted icing for the cherry blossoms and speckle them across the surface.

- Finish off by giving the edges of your fan a gilt-look with some edible gold lustre dust.

# THE NIGHT CIRCUS

## ERIN MORGENSTERN

This fantastical novel takes the feuding of rival magicians to epic new heights. When Prospero the Enchanter and the mysterious Mr A.H. pit their young protégées (and star-crossed lovers) against each other, the scene is set for a showdown of magical proportions. With more flair than David Copperfield's famous coif, *The Night Circus* was a hit with fantasy lovers everywhere and drew comparisons to that other popular and brilliant neo-Victorian alt-historical novel, Susanna Clarke's *Jonathan Strange and Mr Norrell*.

In *The Night Circus*, readers are invited into the mysterious world of Le Cirque des Rêves (The Circus of Dreams) which features a blossoming ice garden, daring acrobatic feats and

a cloud maze that transports lost visitors back to where they started. Only open during the magical hours of sunset to sunrise, the circus is the perfect setting for a doomed love story – and the kind of place readers (myself included) love returning to with each subsequent reading, simply to experience that ambience of wonder and enchantment again.

Magical rivalries are nothing new of course. One of the most famous real-life face-offs took place between Harry Houdini and his nemesis Cirnoc (real name Paul Conrich). Cirnoc once challenged Houdini while he was on stage to prove that he was the real 'king' of handcuff escapes. After escaping from a notoriously challenging pair, Houdini turned the tables on Cirnoc, who failed miserably and had to concede defeat. Then there's the well-known rivalry between P. T. Selbit, inventor of the 'Sawing through a Woman in a Box Illusion' and magician Horace Goldin. The two men were so eager to outdo each other they once flooded the stage with fake blood mid-performance, which must have been quite a surprise for those in the front-row 'splash zone'.

If you want to perform your own bit of baking magic, consider filling your cookie with edible stars. You'll need three cookies of the same shape. Here's how to do it:

- Cut three hat-shaped cookies out of your rolled-out dough.

- Cut a small square out of the middle cookie.

- Bake the three cookies at 180°C for 18 minutes, turning once.

- When the cookies are dry, pipe and flood the first and allow to dry.

- Assemble your cookies by gluing the middle biscuit to the bottom one with stiff icing, then fill the hollow with stars. Place the iced cookie on top to finish.

# THE GREAT GATSBY

## F. SCOTT FITZGERALD

Not many people have much sympathy for Jay Gatsby, the brooding anti-hero of Fitzgerald's moody commentary on America's loss of innocence. He's the kind of guy we love to read about but would find intolerable if he rolled up outside in his Merc. He's the ultimate creepy ex-boyfriend, hanging around to remind you what you missed out on.

Don't get me wrong, I love the whole Gatsby aesthetic: the flappers, the prohibition booze, the vacuous parties on Long Island paid for by Daddy's trust-fund. There's a delicious opulence and decadence in the book (especially the party scenes) that makes me want to cut my hair into a bob and Charleston 'til dawn. But then Fitzgerald throws in the contrast of the slum areas outside Rhode Island and exposes how one-sided the whole business is; desperate depression on the one hand, filthy opulence on the other. Both Nick Carraway (useless enabler) and Jay Gatsby (hopeless dreamer) really rub me up the wrong way.

Daisy, on the other hand, is a girl after my own heart. Unlike Gatsby, who tries to mould himself into some kind of unreachable ideal, Daisy goes straight for the Cartier and doesn't feel a bit bad about it. She never apologises for who she is or what she wants. Is it her fault Gatsby puts her on an impossibly high pedestal? Not at all! It might be unfashionable, but make like a mint julep and be a Daisy; throw your troubles to the wind and let some man do the worrying for you.

I think Daisy would appreciate these flapper girl cookies with their oh-so-chic wink and stylish cloche hats. Don't forget to add a dash of edible gold to embellish your decorations!

# STARDUST

## NEIL GAIMAN

One night when I was four, my dad went outside and brought me back a star. He told me he'd climbed into the sky to get it and I totally believed him. The star was slightly tacky and covered in sticky glitter, which got all over my hands, but I loved it anyway. It was only years later that I worked out he'd gone into the garage and cut it out of cardboard, then sprayed it with glitter glue.

Not many authors can claim the kind of rock star legend status that British author Neil Gaiman has achieved over twenty years of writing fiction for children and adults. *Stardust*, one of his first forays into adult fantasy fiction, crackles with the macabre and the whimsical. In Gaiman's books, anything is possible. A woman with the face of a cat is magically imprisoned as a bird. A market appears once every nine years to act as a bridge between human and fairy traders. A boy falls in love with a star, who has a quest of her own to complete before she can help him find his true love's desire.

The best books remind us why we fell in love with reading and *Stardust* is perfect for those adults who never wanted to grow up. You know, the ones who still believe their dad went outside on a shivery cold night to fetch them the stars …

Make your own *Stardust* cookies by cutting out your shapes with a star cutter and outlining and flooding them with yellow-tinted icing. Paint with edible gold lustre dust mixed with rose spirit and allow to dry.

# THE LION, THE WITCH AND THE WARDROBE

## C.S. LEWIS

Oh, to live in the world of Narnia and the Spare 'Oom, where gentle fauns take refuge from the bitter snow at home and hunker down with tea with crumpets. A place where a child can be a king or a queen and a wise old lion is always on hand to offer advice and save the day. A place where, of course, it's always winter but never Christmas.

This fact puzzled me when I was a kid, coming from the Southern hemisphere where it in fact *is* winter but never Christmas. Regardless of the geographic confusion, *The Lion the Witch and the Wardrobe* remains one of my favourite C. S. Lewis tales of all times (with *Prince Caspian* coming a close second). It's always a pleasure to return to the first in the Narnia series and even more enjoyable to come up with cookies that pay homage to this charming – and edgy – bit of childish delight.

Rectangular cookie cutters are slightly harder to find than round but I do recommend you snaffle them if you find them; you want to get the proportions exactly right for these wardrobe cookies. As far as decorating goes, I recommend looking up some images of wardrobe doors and drawing a basic design onto paper first, eliminating any unnecessary lines which will clutter the look.

After the cookies are baked and cooled, outline and flood in brown-tinted icing. Draw the details on free-hand using a 1.5 mm tip with black-tinted icing. It's a good idea to practice first on a bit of paper if you're not feeling confident. It took me a couple of goes to get these right. Another alternative is to draw the design onto your cookie with an edible ink pen, then simply follow the lines. Don't forget a light dusting of icing sugar for the snow!

# JANE EYRE

## CHARLOTTE BRONTË

Charlotte Brontë was a woman ahead of her time. Centuries before Twitter transformed the image of a little bluebird into the universal symbol for stalking your ex, Brontë was using birds to convey the repression of women in her beloved British proto-feminist classic. Birds play a huge role in Brontë's book. The dove, the nightingale, the eagle, the robin. Each feathery friend within the novel's pages forms part of Jane's intriguing persona and her desire to be free.

When Jane first arrives at Thornfield Hall, she's a shy little thing, caged by her own social standing. By the time she shows up at Ferndean Manor at the end, she's a badass eagle come back to rescue Rochester from his doldrums. The book's feminist leanings are most explicit in the speech Jane delivers to Rochester in the garden, where she proclaims she is his equal and refuses to be the restrained, delicate model of propriety that society demands of her. Go Jane! Speaking of Rochester (and let's be honest, playing imaginary casting director in charge of which current Hollywood heart-throb should be allowed to scowl at Jane is half the fun of waiting for a new film or TV adaptation), it's always interesting when rereading *Jane Eyre* to see how the story frames him as the victim. What about the madwoman in the attic? Poor Bertha never stood a chance, as Jean Rhys so eloquently explores in *Wide Sargasso Sea*. Like Jane, she is a woman trapped in a cage, but in the end they both achieve freedom.

Release your inner Jane with these bluebird cookies. Here's how to get the look:

- Once baked and cooled, outline and flood your cookie in blue-tinted icing.

- Allow to dry then mix up some edible silver paint with a dab of rose spirit.

- Using a fine-tipped brush, paint the feathers onto the bird, building up the layers until dry. Rose spirit dries really quickly so work fast!

- Pipe on the eye and beak using a 1.5 mm tip and black and yellow icing.

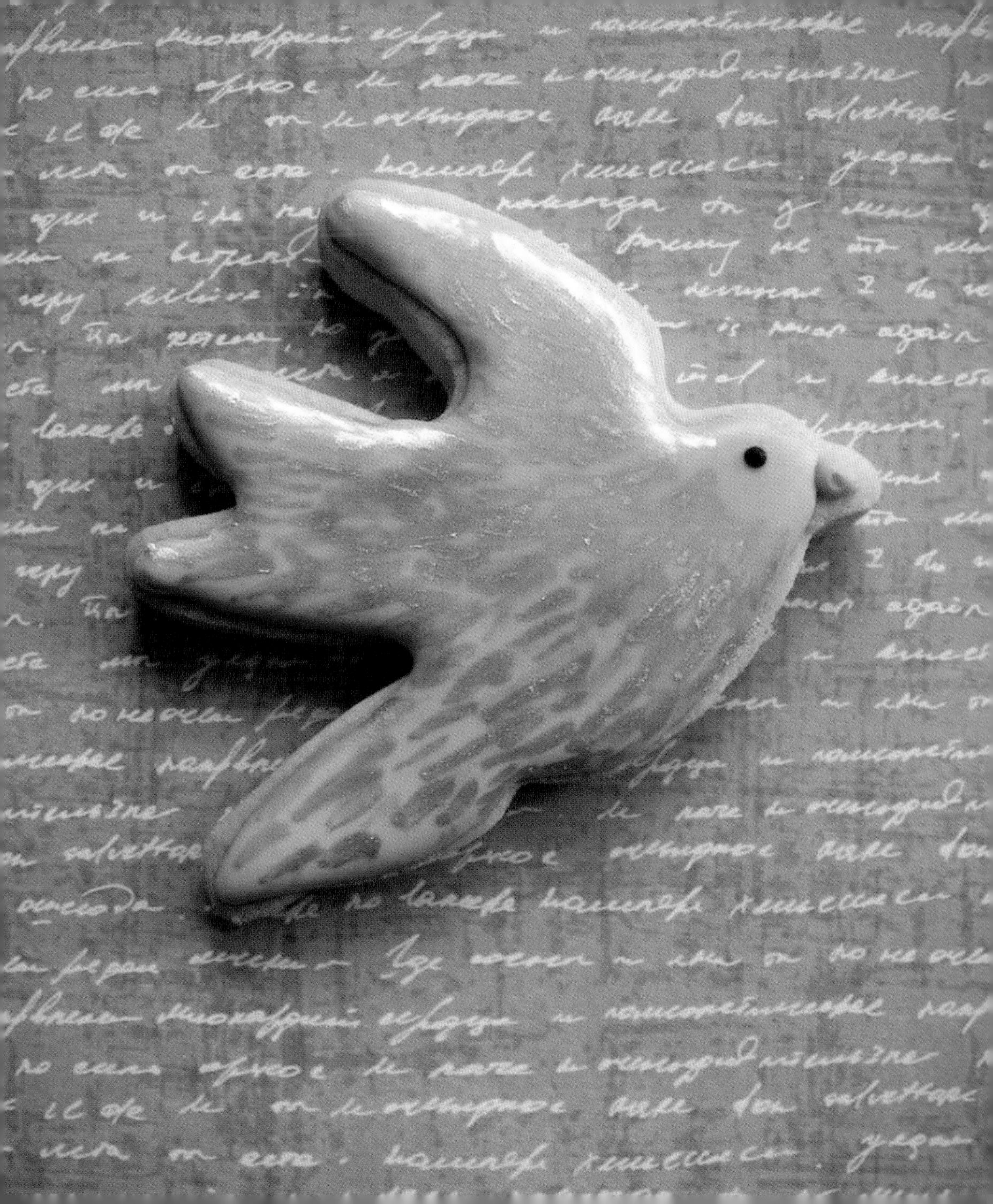

# THE VIRGIN SUICIDES

### JEFFREY EUGENIDES

Ah, the trope of the mysterious dead girl who will forever haunt the memories of the boy who loved her. It's a concept as old as the hills, but Eugenides does something really interesting with it in this brooding, darkly funny commentary about intergenerational trauma and American culture.

Suicide, of course, is nothing new in literature. Ever since Anna Karenina threw herself in front of that steam train at the end of Tolstoy's classic, authors have probed the human compulsion to self-destruct. What makes *The Virgin Suicides* so unique is the mystery of the girls, the way we never know quite what they're thinking.

All we learn about them is the miscellany we glean from their interest in the usual teenage preoccupations – their love of music, hairstyles and clothing. While this is going on, the town's beloved elm trees begin to die from a mysterious disease, an allegory for the insidious way that suicide can creep into families and cross generations. As the girls lose their freedom and become prisoners in their home, their lives become one long daydream, a kaleidoscope of hair products, sleeping aids and unmentionables.

I tried to capture the dreamy essence of Eugenides' novel and embellished my biscuits with flowers using a technique called brush embroidery. Here's how you do it:

- Pipe and flood your cookie first with your desired colour. Allow to dry fully for at least 8 hours.

- Prepare some stiff white icing and pop it in an icing bag with a 2 mm tip.

- Pipe a curved line onto your iced cookie.

- Using a flat-edged brush and some rose spirit, brush carefully inwards. Repeat until you've created all the various petals.

# LORD OF THE FLIES

## WILLIAM GOLDING

Everyone has someone in their life that they couldn't imagine being stranded on a desert island with. Maybe it's your Uncle Rick, who has bad breath and wears terrible knitted jumpers. Maybe it's that friend from high school who tells the most mortifying dad jokes at parties. You'd be hard pressed, though, to be trapped on an island with anyone worse than the bunch of feral teenagers in William Golding's classic drama *Lord of the Flies*.

This book is hea-vy, but its original concept and themes have been consistently reinvented and parodied in popular culture and can be found everywhere from the popular reality television experiment *Big Brother* (and every other spin-off, like that other reality show set on a big island) to *The Simpsons*, which dedicated a full half-hour episode to their take on it (who could forget Ralph Wiggum in those cat whiskers?), not forgetting of course that Suzanne Collins's *The Hunger Games* has given *Lord of the Flies* a run for its money. Golding's depiction of adolescents getting drunk of their own power and rampaging over everything is pretty much how I spent my teenage years and it's clear Golding had a lot of real life material to work with, too, as he worked as a schoolmaster at a prestigious school before he wrote the book.

My favourite part of the story is the conch shell, as only the person holding the shell is allowed to speak. I tried this with my kids but they just laughed. You can make your own conch shell cookies this way:

- Pipe and flood ivory-tinted icing then pipe white dots with a 1.5 mm tip straight onto the wet surface.

- Once dry, use the brush embroidery technique on page 105 to achieve the scalloped edge look.

# THE NORTH WATER

## IAN MCGUIRE

Polar bears feature heavily in this bloody neo-Victorian novel about a rigged quest to the Arctic whaling waters. I feel sort of dirty admitting this, but I loved it in all its gruesome glory and so of course, I had to make cookies to match.

This is not a book for the faint-hearted. Slaughter of both the human and animal variety abounds but there's an extraordinary sense of place that I just can't let go of and the polar bears were so well-described I felt as if I was standing on a whaler in freezing Arctic waters, looking through the bars at the poor creatures as they were transported back to England.

What I loved best about this book was the contrast of the brutality of whaling with the supposedly upright morals of 19th century English upper-crust society. It made me feel very uncomfortable, but I really liked what it had to say about the violence humans perpetrate on the environment – and each other.

If you want to give your polar bears a clever, three dimensional texture, here are some tips:

- Pipe and flood your base coat and allow to dry for at least 8 hours.

- Prepare some stiff piping icing and pop it in a bag with a 2 mm tip.

- Draw wavy lines across the bear's body.

- Using a small dry brush, 'dab' the icing all over the cookie. You can be as messy as you like; in fact I think it looks better that way!

- When your 'fur' has dried, pop on the polar bear's eyes with two dots of black icing.

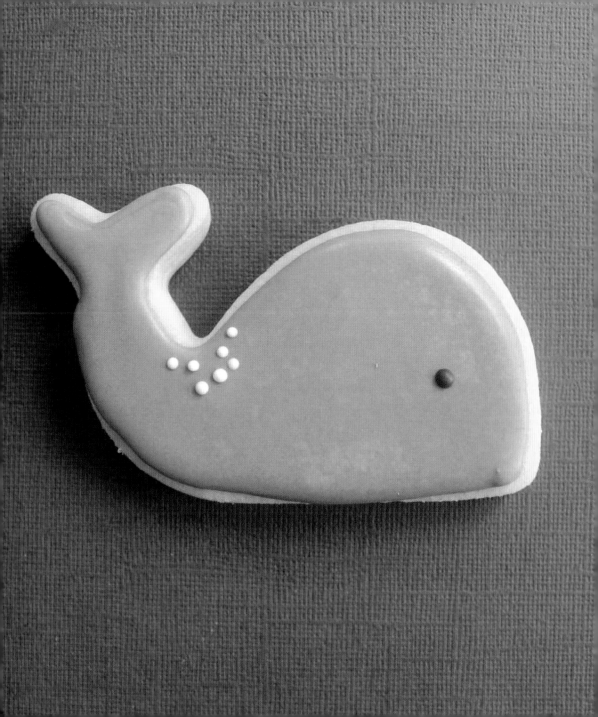

# THE ROSIE PROJECT

## GRAEME SIMSION

Rom com holds a very special place in the hearts of literature lovers. A good one gives us hope. It helps us laugh at our own *faux pas* (like the piece of parsley stuck between our teeth on that date with the crush) and after all the soul-searching, we know there's going to be a guaranteed feel-good ending. But what exactly makes a rom com stand out from the many, many others? What makes a rom com a classic?

I give you *The Rosie Project*.

This book is such a blast. Funny, irreverent and replete with genetic in-jokes (my favourite kind), it's no wonder readers love it so much. What makes it so delightful is how relatable Don Tillman is. Everybody knows a Don – he's the awkward guy in the cubicle near the windows at work who can't quite make eye contact, or that guy at the party rearranging the food on his plate so the colours don't touch. If you don't know a Don, well, I have some news: you *are* the Don. That's okay, though. This book is proof that even those of us with quirky, eccentric habits can find true love and somebody to laugh with.

The Jacket Incident is my favourite of all Don's schemes. If you've read the book, you'll know why. These Gore-Tex jacket cookies are Don Tillman approved. Lightweight, slightly sweet and a little bit surprising, just like Don himself.

# YEAR OF WONDERS

### GERALDINE BROOKS

This book needs to come with a warning: you may be turned off eating apples forever! A deliciously sad novel about the plague, Geraldine Brooks's first foray into fiction was a huge hit but may have left apple farmers fuming. You see, the plague, according to the novel's heroine Anna Frith, apparently has a very distinctive smell – sweet and pervasive, like the aroma of rotting apples. Gross.

Brooks was inspired to write the book after visiting the 'plague village' of Eyam, England, now famous because its inhabitants chose to stay and quarantine themselves rather than risk spreading the disease to others. Although the last 'great plague' of 1665 to 1666 carried off over 100,000 people, you can relive the horror by diving into Brooks's fine historical work. One of the things I loved reading about were all the snake-oil charms people came up with to sell to people during their grief: Plague water, spells, herbals. Those 17th century charlatans sure knew their market.

Combined with this fascinating insight into old-school quackery, Brooks's novel features one of the most compelling and interesting characters of modern literature, Anna Frith, a widow whose ideas on the nature of God and the subjugation of women are challenged in the aftermath of tragedy.

If your stomach is still feeling delicate, these apple-shaped cookies provide a welcome alternative to fruit.

- Pipe and flood the outline of the apple in red-tinted icing.

- Fill in the middle section with ivory-tinted icing.

- Wait until the middle section is fully dry before piping on the black 'pips' with a fine 1.5 mm tip.

# FOAL'S BREAD

## GILLIAN MEARS

You have to hand it to Australians: aside from the Americans, we probably have more depictions of horses in our literature than any other culture. We're frothing mad horse fans. Even Banjo Paterson, well-known Bush poet, author and legendary creator of that sometimes cringeworthy ballad 'Waltzing Matilda', had a particular affinity for horses, which always found their way into his work. The Silver Brumby series by Elyne Mitchell, which my sister Nette and I read when we were children, is in fact the reason behind Nette's lifelong pony obsession. I'll never forget spending hours trapped in the car with her from Sydney to Adelaide while she cried buckets and begged my dad for a silver brumby of her own. When he asked her where she planned to keep it, she suggested the garage.

Even as adults we can't get enough of these majestic beasts, and the mythology of their link with the Australian landscape inhabits our favourite fiction. In Gillian Mears's *Foal's Bread*, the connection between two lovers is sealed when he gifts her a piece of 'foal's bread', a bit of gristle which portends a horse's success on the high-jump at the show. They also share some of Auntie Rolie's gingernut cookies and dip them in a cup of tea.

A biscuit in tea is as Australian as it gets, so I recommend having a strong cuppa on hand if you decide to make these iced thoroughbreds, inspired by Mears's beautiful tale of redemption and hope, an Aussie family saga as tender and classic as any jolly swagman's colonial tale.

# ANNE OF GREEN GABLES

## L.M. MONTGOMERY

L. M. Montgomery's 'Anne with an E' is arguably literature's most iconic redhead. Feisty, smart and fiercely loyal, she's the best friend I always wanted when I was a teenager. Some girls have crushes on Mr Darcy – I had a crush on Anne Shirley. She's the lonely girl's go-to, the intelligent student's idol. When she smashes that slate over Gilbert's head, you can't help but do a little fist pump in solidarity. And when she says that being smart is better than being pretty? Girl, you are speaking my language.

In fact, the redheaded snippet remains so popular that every year, hundreds of pilgrims make the journey to Prince Edward Island to visit her 'house' and pay respects to the Lake of Shining Waters where Anne and her bestie Diana exchanged secret vows to love each other for as long as they lived. And of course there's dreamboat Gilbert, although he never quite came alive for me in the way Anne did. I'm still glad L. M. Montgomery didn't pull a Louisa May Alcott and marry Anne off to that blue-stocking snob from Kingston. Gilbert was her true love and Montgomery gifted her plucky heroine with the happy ending she herself never achieved.

I simply had to immortalise my favourite redhaired character with these bright and cheerful daffodil cookies. To get the look:

- Outline and flood your cookie in yellow-tinted icing.

- Use the brush embroidery technique to pipe the flowery centres.

- Once dry, dab the edges of the centre with bright yellow dye mixed with rose spirit.

# THE GERMAN GIRL

## ARMANDO LUCAS CORREA

Many people see passenger liners as places of transit, a bridge between the old world and the new. This unique experience takes a tragic twist in Armando Lucas Correa's novel, which chronicles the ill-fated journey of the transatlantic liner *St Louis* through the eyes of a young Jewish girl, Hannah Rosenthal. Fleeing the persecution of the Nazi regime in 1939, Hannah and her parents join others on board the ship, expecting to disembark in Cuba, but their excitement quickly sours as the ship is turned away from that port, and every other, and the liner soon becomes a floating crypt. Correa pays tribute to those poor souls in this sobering story about war, hope and the human condition.

Of all the passenger liner tragedies in popular culture, the best known is of course the White Star's *Titanic* but the success of Correa's book has recently thrown light on the forgotten passenger ship *St Louis*. A German ocean liner, she set out in May 1939 and soon became embroiled in a political and humanitarian crisis when Jewish passengers fleeing the Holocaust were denied entry at every port.

With an eye to the recent horrors in Syria, Correa's book seems more relevant than ever and, cute cookies aside, it's one that everyone should read to prevent such a tragedy ever occurring again. These liner cookies were made using a custom cutter but any steamship cutter will do.

- Outline and flood the bottom section first in black icing.

- Outline and flood the top half in bright white icing once the bottom has dried.

- Use grey icing in a piping bag fitted with a 1.5 mm tip to add the decorative stripes and the windows.

# CHARLOTTE'S WEB

## E.B. WHITE

'Terrific'. 'Radiant'. 'Humble'.

Charlotte the spider sure knows how to pare back her adjectives. This really is one of the most brilliant children's stories and it's about an adorable pig named Wilbur whose best friend is a spider with writing aspirations so it's a total winner, in my books! Reading this book as both a child and as an adult is an interesting experience. As a kid, I got the not-so-subtle subtext about friendship (be friends with both the rats and the spiders in your life, because they're often the ones who save your ass!). But it was only when I read the book as an adult that I understood the sadness and sacrifice of Charlotte's gift.

Charlotte A. Cavatica is a barn spider. Like many spiders, she's nocturnal and an orb weaver, ordinary and unremarkable, and was, in fact, based on a real-life spider E. B. White stumbled across in a barn. He popped her into the book he was writing, thereby immortalising her forever and probably saving a few arachnids from death-by-shoe into the bargain.

These Charlotte cookies are a little complicated, but well worth the effort. You'll need a web-shaped cookie cutter to make them. Here are a few tips to get you started:

- To make the web pattern, outline and flood your cookie in white icing, then draw thin circles in grey icing straight on top.

- Using the wet-on-wet technique, drag a toothpick through the icing, to create the 'spokes' in the web. Allow to dry.

- Pipe the spiders onto the web with brown icing using a 1.5 mm tip. Allow to dry before piping on the legs. Dust the spiders in bronze lustre dust and cover the whole lot in edible shimmer spray.

# THE OTHER BOLEYN GIRL

## PHILIPPA GREGORY

Divorced, beheaded, died, divorced, beheaded, survived. Not many kings have left behind the legacy of a mnemonic rhyme to remember them by. Yet that's exactly what King Henry VIII of England did (in addition to the persistent but untrue rumour that he wrote 'Greensleeves'). Readers have been lapping up stories about his maniacal wife-killing ever since.

*The Other Boleyn Girl* riffs on the more familiar story of Anne Boleyn, Henry's second wife, but provides a twist – it's Mary, Anne's sister, who is the heroine of this tale. Lesser known than her infamous sister, Mary was also one of the king's mistresses but,

unlike Anne, Mary managed to escape with her head and went on to marry and have children.

Of course, monarchs aren't exactly known for their fidelity, so Mary probably considered herself lucky to be cast aside when Henry took up with her sister. King Henry I left behind no less than 20 illegitimate children, while the French Sun King himself, Louis XIV, had a secret mistress who tried to escape him by joining a convent, only to find herself returned to court and bestowed with the dubious title of 'official mistress' alongside all his unofficial ones. The reigning house of Windsor has undeniably delivered its fair share of scandal, too.

It seems we just can't get enough of crazy dynastic capers. If you feeling like getting your royal on, these crown cookies are simple but magisterial.

Add some bling in the form of sweet, sugary cachous balls to make your crown stand out from the crowd.

# THE SECRET GARDEN

## FRANCIS HODGSON BURNETT

*The Secret Garden* is one of those books that is fixed firmly in the orphan-in-need-of-rescuing school of literature. The story of a wealthy girl orphan brought from India to live in a mysterious English mansion who unites an estranged family might seem a bit twee in our celebrity-obsessed era where young girls are more likely to identify with Kim Kardashian and Taylor Swift than sour-faced Mary Lennox. But the book is a lovely testament to a time when things were allowed to take their time to flourish and grow. With each passing season, Mary's secret garden becomes a sanctuary from the pressures of the world and a place where children can be themselves and say what's in their hearts when words cannot suffice. Perhaps a reaction to that old adage 'children should be seen and not heard', the garden is also a place for them to play, an idea that was quite revolutionary at the time, as children were viewed as tiny adults, punishable by force when they misbehaved, rather than creatures who needed nourishing. Something that always surprises me about *The Secret Garden* is its allusions to the Victorian art of communing and communicating through flowers. Among the many customs of the Victorian era, none were perhaps as enchanting as giving flowers to another person which conveyed secret wishes. Here are a few of my faves:

- Red tulips: perfect love
- Red roses: desire and love
- Forget-me-nots: true love
- Cedar: I live for thee

To make these robin cookies, I outlined and piped the top and the bottom halves separately then added the details (eye and beak) with a 1.5 mm tip. I used red food dye mixed with rose spirit to paint the robin's breast feathers.

# REBECCA

## DAPHNE DU MAURIER

Quite possibly my favourite book of all time, du Maurier's classic tale of romantic suspense was actually conceived while the author was living in Egypt with her husband, an army officer. Although she predicted *Rebecca* wouldn't be of much interest, it went on to enthral readers everywhere and inspire movie and TV adaptations, most notably the Hitchcock version starring Joan Fontaine (as the nameless 'I') and the brilliant Judith Anderson (as the utterly loopy Mrs Danvers).

I first read this book as a teenager and completely lost myself in its dark Gothic atmosphere and that sense of yearning for the past that we can never return to. Although ostensibly a mystery, I like to think of it more as a coming-of-age story

about a young woman finding her feet and her own courage. The ending is a total firecracker, too; perhaps one of the best ever, since it leaves the reader wanting more.

Manderley, the house at the heart of the story, was based on the real castle Menabilly, which Daphne had visited as a girl. Covered in a thick trellis of ivy, the house was a dream and with the proceeds of *Rebecca*, du Maurier finally achieved her lifelong dream of leasing it and living within its beautiful walls.

One of my favourite scenes in the novel is when the narrator finds all of Rebecca's old correspondence, scrawled over with her name with the imposing capital R and all the flourishes. That scene inspired these cookies!

To make beautiful *Rebecca* biscuits, you'll need to do the following:

- Pipe and flood your rectangular cookies with midnight or navy blue icing.

- Using a 1.5 mm tip and yellow-tinted icing, mark out the areas where you want your text to go by piping lines across the surface.

- Pipe in the author's name.

- Using a 1.5 mm tip and red-tinted icing, pipe the title.

- Add yellow swirls and flourishes with your piping icing.

# GREEN EGGS AND HAM

## DR. SEUSS

From Lewis Carroll's brillig Jabberwocky to Edward Lear's runcible spoons, nonsense verse remains a delightful literary distraction even as it confuses readers everywhere. Sometimes naughty, sometimes merely humorous, limericks and rhymes have satirised everything that deserves to be laughed at and many things that don't. Some suggest the election of American President Trump was the reason behind an explosion of online satirical poetry and verse. One Twitter account I follow is completely devoted to daily limericks which summarise all the misdemeanours, revelations and random midnight tweetings in a glorious confection of rhyme. Not since the Restoration in the 17th century, when people openly flamed their opponents in the daily rag, have witticisms been so artfully employed to expose the humour behind closed doors.

Of all the poets we read as children, there is probably none so prolific or pleasurable as Dr. Seuss and none so well-known as his iconic *Green Eggs and Ham*. A fabulist tale of imagination and ovum, *Green Eggs and Ham* is the tale of Sam, who follows around a miserable nameless character, trying to convince him to try his food. Of course, when the poor old creature does taste the green eggs, he's smitten. The moral of the story is about trying things you don't like the idea of, but I don't think you'll have a problem substituting green eggs and ham for their cookie counterparts!

- I used a fork cutter, and a round cutter for the eggs.

- Use edible silver dust mixed with rose spirit to give your cutlery a realistic steel shine.

- These cookies make cute presents popped in a Chinese take-away container box lined with a red and white checked napkin. *Bon appetit*!

# ALIAS GRACE

## MARGARET ATWOOD

Murderess, murderess.

I must admit to becoming obsessed with Grace Marks after reading this book. I used Atwood's notes to track down everything I could about her, but after all that, I still couldn't work out if she'd done the deed or not. That mystery woven through the story is just one part, though, of what makes *Alias Grace* such a brilliant piece of fiction. Aside from the obvious question of whether shedunnit or not, *Alias Grace* features some amazing metaphors and motifs that had me scuttling off to research quilt patterns.

Grace's pointed comment to Doctor Simon about beds being a symbol of woman's sexuality is so

very true! Quilts teach us about how the world works, especially for women, and the tradition of making them and passing down that knowledge is probably why quilting has survived and flourished, even with the advent of so much digital distraction. Grace's favourite quilt is the Tree of Life, so I knew I'd have to make some quilt cookies in her style, although I used butter and icing instead of needles and applique. I can imagine serving these to Grace while taking tea in the Governor's mansion. The perfect afternoon snack for a murderess?

Here's how to make your own Tree of Life cookies:

- Outline and flood your cookie with a base of ivory-tinted icing. Allow to dry.

- Copy out a tree design you like onto a piece of paper, then use the paper as a guide to help you pipe on the finer details with a 1.5 mm tip. I used a variety of colours for the tree; brown for the bark, dusty pink and pale pink for the blossoms, forest green and electric green for the leaves.

- Finish off by adding a few birds in electric blue and some grass in leaf green.

# WATER FOR ELEPHANTS

## SARA GRUEN

In 2006, I lost my heart to a book and an elephant. The book was by Sara Gruen and the elephant's name was Rosie. Rosie is the absolute stand-out star of this dazzling and romantic novel about the dying grandeur of America's last circus trains. Stubborn but sweet-tempered, she only obeys her trainer Jacob because he speaks to her in her native language – Polish.

Elephants as characters are nothing new – Suki, the Saggy Baggy Elephant, has been charming children for decades while Joseph Conrad's depiction of elephant slaughter in *Heart of Darkness* just keeps on horrifying. But Rosie is something else. The depression-era circus that she is part of provides a fabulous backdrop to this tale of romance and the importance of following your dreams. According to Gruen's notes, she studied elephant behaviour and spent a lot of time with an elephant-handler at the Kansas Zoo. Rosie leaps off the page as a larger than life character. Her partiality to buckets of gin and her wicked sense of humour transcend the usual attributes of non-speaking characters but like most elephants, Rosie has a good memory, and the important role she plays at the novel's climax makes her an unforgettable symbol of power and a reminder that we should always treat animals with humility and kindness.

To make a Rosie cookie:

- Draw the shape of Rosie's cushion first in edible ink.

- Outline and flood her body in grey-tinted icing and allow to dry.

- Outline and flood the cushion in yellow icing.

- Pipe on the details (eyes, tail and ears) using a piping bag with a 1.5 mm tip.

- Brush some edible gold paint mixed with rose spirit onto the seat for a little circus glam.

# DAUGHTER OF FORTUNE

## ISABEL ALLENDE

Isabel Allende is one of the world's most beloved and eccentric authors. Refusing to start her books on any date other than the 8th of January (a tradition she began in 1981), Allende is the queen of magic realism and Chilean storytelling and *Daughter of Fortune* is a heady concoction of myth and colonial entanglements. Riddled with allusions to Allende's Chilean heritage, the book weaves a story of romance and broken dreams with the mystery of secret parentage.

I love how magic occurs so randomly within Allende's novels and how love is entwined with loss. Then there's the superstition which wafts through the book like perfume. My love of Allende's books has crossed the ocean thanks to social media and I now exchange reviews with a few good Chilean pals. If you're a newcomer to Allende and Chilean superstition, let me give you a taste of what to expect:

- Tuesday the 13th is an unlucky day in Chilean culture.

- If you're a ginger, watch out; pinching a redhead brings good luck.

- Don't spill the salt or a piano will fall on you (slight exaggeration but bad luck in some form is guaranteed).

- Hold your glass tightly at a wedding! Dropping a glass means your marriage is destined to fail.

In the tradition of sepia-toned daguerreotypes, I recommend having a go at these old-fashioned girl-in-a-bonnet cookies. I used two shades of ivory, one light and one dark. Sometimes simplicity is key.

# CHOCOLAT

## JOANNE HARRIS

If you love chocolate, French music, chocolate, children, chocolate and stories about towns which are transformed by mysterious strangers (and chocolate), then this is the book for you. Although *Chocolat* has much more going for it than its delectable title would suggest. This is a book about the alchemy of friendship and connection, but you already know that if you've read it and fallen under its delicious chocolatey spell. Warning: do not read without a box of treats on hand or you might find yourself nibbling the couch arms.

Aside from the time I read *James and the Giant Peach* as a child and snuck out to raid the fruit bowl in the wee hours of the morning, I can't recall a time when I've been so hungry while reading a novel. After finishing the book, I actually took myself off to do a chocolate making course, inspired by Vianne's magical ability to transform cacao and sugar into edible art.

Please don't expect me to bring out a chocolate book any time soon, though: I can now confirm that for the near future, I'll be sticking to biscuits. Chocolate is so much harder to work with than people realise. First there's the tempering, then the moulds, then the chocolate has to be left alone to set before you can eat it which, excuse my French, is not the damn point!

To comfort myself, I made these guitars inspired by my favourite *Chocolat* character, Roux. Yes, they're biscuits. Not a bit of chocolate in sight (except for the bought ones).

# THE CINDERELLA MURDERS

## MARY HIGGINS CLARK

John Waters assures us that it's impossible to commit a crime while reading a good book. I can only conclude that are a lot of lazy serial killers out there, especially if they're reading crime, because this genre of fiction continues to be more popular than ever, with hundreds of new authors added each year to an ever-growing pool of amazing and talented crime-plotters. It seems readers can't get enough of reading about people being maimed, shot, drugged, eaten, torn apart by vicious dogs or shoved into wheelie bins.

What is it about crime that makes it so damned fascinating? I suspect it's got something to do with that old Nosy Parker habit of wanting to know what your neighbours are up to. Let's face it, who hasn't contemplated whether Susan from next door is actually the Blue Alphabet Murderer who cuts ransom notes out of the *Sunday Telegraph*?

Marry Higgins Clark is the absolute queen of crime and *The Cinderella Murders* picks up on one of the genre's most loved combos – TV starlet found murdered. With a possible cult connection and a murderer who seems to crave the spotlight, this is crime escapism at its best. There's a reason crime novels are regularly referred to as 'cosies' and it's not just because everything at the end is wrapped up neatly. It's a hint for you to put your kettle on, curl up in your reading chair and enjoy one of these stiletto cookies with your tea.

# GONE WITH THE WIND

## MARGARET MITCHELL

Well, fiddle-dee-dee, if it isn't one of literature's most celebrated heroines immortalised in a cookie version of her infamous sprigged muslin dress. Scarlett O'Hara has only two things she really cares about in life: Scarlett and Tara, the property plantation left to her by her father.

With a first edition weighing in at over 1000 pages ('Outrageous!' I can imagine Scarlett saying), this classic tome of plantation fiction offers a fresh perspective on the 'fragile' heroine. Despite all her losses, it's hard not to admire Scarlett's plucky courage and enjoy watching her transform from a spoilt, arrogant teenager, changed by the ravages of the Civil War, to a grown woman

who is … okay, still spoilt and arrogant, but also tough as nails and more aware of how her choices affect others. The book differs slightly from the movie, but it's almost impossible to read the book now without imagining Vivien Leigh in that role, wearing that damn dress. Every time she lifts her eyes and they flash with that brilliant emerald green, I feel equal parts envy and admiration. Mostly, I just want that 17-inch waist (the smallest in three counties, we are told) and that wacky crinoline that's so ostentatious she has to turn sideways to squeeze through the door.

The sad truth is you probably won't have a 17-inch waist after eating these cookies. The good news is Scarlett O'Hara, despite being a vain creature, was more attractive because of her confidence and charm than actual looks would suggest. Author Margaret Mitchell tells us Scarlett's not a beautiful girl, but men seldom notice because she's so engaging and spirited. That's something for us all to aspire to. Alternatively, you could always bake up a batch of these dress cookies, sure to catch the roving eye of an Ashley or two. Here's how to get the look:

- Outline and flood your cookie in white icing. Quickly pipe on the 'ferns' using a flood-consistency icing with a 1.5 mm tip.

- Outline and flood the waist sash.

- When completely dry, fill a piping bag with a mixture of stiff green and white icing, then fit it with a ribbon tip and gently 'wiggle' it across the neckline to achieve the flouncy embellishments.

# LITTLE WOMEN

## LOUISA MAY ALCOTT

When I meet new potential friends, I like to give them the March test. Yes, that's right: I ask them which *Little Women* character they most identify with. You see, you can tell a lot about a person from which March girl they relate to.

Amy? Self-absorbed but gifted. Likes limes (in her martini).

Jo? Angsty and creative. Loyal to a fault but can't see when her best friend's in love with her.

Meg? Domestic and sweet. Enjoys the finer things in life and maxes out her credit card.

Beth? Doomed.

It's a really good indicator of whether we'll be a good match. It's not often that Jos and Amys run together, although I did once know a pair who teamed up to undertake a school fundraiser and collectively coerced more money out of the parents than any other year in the school's history. I suspect Jo played 'good cop' to Amy's 'bad'. Amazing what literature can teach us about ourselves.

What can also be taught is the method to making these adorable scissor cookies, inspired by Louisa May Alcott's lovely tale about the too-good-to-be-true March sisters. Although these cookies are on the small side, they make dainty bite-sized snacks to eat with your thick German coffee (Professor Bhaer style).

- Use a 1.5 mm tip to pipe on the handles one by one, allowing them to dry in between so the icing doesn't all blend together.

- Pipe on the blades and allow to dry.

- Paint a little silver lustre dust mixed with rose spirit onto the blades to give them a realistic gleam.

- Eat and enjoy.

# THE GOLDEN COMPASS

## PHILIP PULLMAN

Not since Jiminy Cricket played smug conscience to cheeky Pinocchio has there been such a harmonious pairing of animals and humans quite like 12-year-old Lyra Belacqua and her shape-shifting daemon Pantalaimon. Fighting the good fight against a collective of evildoers, the pair enlist the help of friends including the formidable armoured bear Iorek Byrnison.

Known as panserbjørne, the armoured bears are a race of polar-bear like creatures who believe their armour is an extension of their souls. Iorek becomes Lyra's lifelong friend after she frees him from his human masters and helps him defeat the bear king. As is often the case in epic children's fiction, the corruption of the adult human world, with its emphasis on power, is more threatening than the monsters Lyra and her friends must face. Themes of friendship and loyalty, bravery and courage raise the stakes in this classic children's novel.

Polar bears are no strangers to mythology and mystical belief. In Innuit mythology, Nanuk was master of the bears. Legend said that a bear's spirit must be treated with respect by being offered tokens or the hunter who violated the rules would be unsuccessful in his hunt. No wonder Philip Pullman included them in his bestselling children's book.

I created these panserbjørne cookies using a cutter which was originally meant to be for wombats. If you'd rather go for something a little more majestic, I think any bear cutter would do. The 'armour' is yellow-tinted icing, glazed with edible gold paint and rose spirit.

Noble bear cookies, ready to be devoured.

# GREAT EXPECTATIONS

## CHARLES DICKENS

Although sometimes considered the bane of English students everywhere, there are good reasons why *Great Expectations* is often chosen as one of the best novels of all time. As well as hosting a great many memorable characters, the novel examines themes of wealth and poverty, as well as self-determinism and willpower. Dickens kicks things off with a tense meeting between Pip and a wanted criminal. Then we meet his family and his friends. But when Miss Havisham shows up in her rotting wedding dress, it's game over. No other character has come close to achieving the kind of cult status she commands with just one heel-clap of her mouldy old slippers (if you've encountered her in Jasper Fforde's Thursday Next novels, you'll know she hasn't lost any of her acerbic wit in the years since publication). Her crumbling manor house, Satis House, is based on a real mansion in Dorset where Dickens lived. The word 'satis' is Latin for 'enough'. Clearly, Dickens intended irony; the house and all its rotten insides are most definitely *not* enough for Miss Havisham, whose machinations and manipulations of her ward and Pip would make Machiavelli blush. I think there's a part of me that secretly envies Miss Havisham and I suspect that, if my love life fell apart, I too would end up eating old wedding cake alone in my house. I've never considered myself an Estella, but Havisham is my kind of bird: rich, reclusive and nuttier than a fruitcake. The original introvert.

Wedding cake cookies are very popular amongst cookie lovers for obvious reasons, but I thought I would give these ones a twist and do a 'before' as well as an 'after'. You can choose which one to make, although I recommend offering your friends both and seeing which one they choose. The 'mould' is ivory food dye mixed with rose spirit; paint it straight onto the 'before' version to give your cake that festering feeling. I'm not one for making promises but there is seriously nothing more fun than making rotten wedding cake cookies. Honestly. Try it. I promise you'll love it.

# INTERVIEW WITH THE VAMPIRE

## ANNE RICE

The first book in Anne Rice's famed Vampire Chronicle series, this book is a fangbanger's delight (see *Dead Until Dark* by Charlaine Harris on page 62). Southern Gothic but with a hint of erotica, the book is essentially a historical novel in which an alternative race of beings thrives, feeding off unsuspecting human prey. What sets this book apart from other popular Gothic novels is its tendency to veer into previously unexplored vampire territory.

The story, told from the world-weary Louis's point of view, details how he was made a vamp after his wife died tragically in childbirth, how he survived the centuries (bearing witness to many of history's key events) and how he has learned more about being human from being dead than he ever did while he was alive. These existential underpinnings, similar to those found in Philip K. Dick's science fiction novels, are the novel's strength. By removing the issue of mortality, Louis is given the chance to examine what makes humans behave the way they do, yet for all he learns, he remains nostalgic for a state of existence he can never return to.

It's hardly surprising that Rice herself has a cult following (she once showed up for an event in a life-size coffin in the back of a hearse) and the Vampire Lestat Masquerade Ball held every year in New Orleans attracts wonderful and bizarre fans from all over the globe.

To get the timber look on these coffins, you'll want to use a 1.5 mm tip to pipe black 'planks' of wood on your dried-out brown base coat. Add some swirls and dots to give the timber an authentic 'knotted' look.

These cookies are great for Halloween too, and if you really want to pump up the creep factor, you can add a light dusting of cocoa for that just-crawled-out-of-the-grave aesthetic.

# NEVER LET ME GO

## KAZUO ISHIGURO

Fact: readers love clones.

Although the idea of clones probably reached peak popularity during the heady heyday of 1950s sci-fi schlock, genetic duplication and its fascinating social implications are pervasive and unsettling themes. There are so many questions when a clone appears in a story: Is it good or evil? Will it replace the protagonist or help him on his quest? Is it here to teach humankind a valuable lesson, or destroy us for our hubris?

My clone obsession began when I read Ira Lewin's *The Boys from Brazil* in high school. That book triggered in me a vast number of complex ideas and, to be honest, it probably raised more questions than it answered. But it introduced me to a whole new

world of sci-fi and I've been hooked on clones ever since. Like all genres, there are some bad books about clones and, okay, it can be a little tacky now when a clone conveniently shows up in a novel in a moment of *deus ex machina* (e.g. Ohhh, the *clone* is the murderer! But who's the original and who's the bad clone? Cue confusion and messy process of elimination). But there are also a lot of amazing novels that explore duality and responsibility, and *Never Let Me Go* is one of them.

Tragic, taboo and transcendent, this book has a special place on my keeper shelf. Aside from Ishiguro's beautiful language, what makes this Booker Prize-winning novel so gripping is the way he elevates the mundane to something extraordinary. To Kathy, the book's protagonist, a simple cassette tape, a rare trip to the seaside, and the act of caring for someone as they 'complete' at the end of their short life are all things she accepts as normal … It's only us, the readers, who are horrified by what has befallen her; what we have allowed to happen by our lack of compassion and understanding.

Of course I had to make tape cookies for this one, which made me very nostalgic for cassette cartridges and winding them up with pencils.

- Use a rectangular cookie cutter to punch out your cookies then bake and allow to cool.

- Use an edible ink marker to mark out the plastic edge of your cassette and fill in with black icing.

- Pipe and flood the middle section with orange icing, then allow to set before icing a white rectangle for the label.

- Use an edible ink marker to write on the collection title.

# RECIPES

### MAKES AROUND 16

**250G UNSALTED BUTTER, SOFTENED**

**1 EGG**

**½ TSP SALT**

**1 CUP CASTER SUGAR**

**1 TSP VANILLA ESSENCE**

**6 CUPS FLOUR, PLUS EXTRA FOR ROLLING OUT**

**½ TSP BAKING POWDER**

**STEP 1** Place softened butter and caster sugar in a large bowl and mix until smooth and light in colour (about four minutes).

**STEP 2** Add in vanilla essence and beat in egg, until combined.

**STEP 3** Slowly beat in the baking powder and flour, one cup at a time. After two minutes or so of beating the dough should start pulling away from the edge of the bowl and form a lump. Remove the dough from the bowl and knead it on a lightly floured surface.

**STEP 4** Wrap the dough in plastic wrap and place in fridge for at least four hours.

**STEP 5** Preheat oven to 180°C (355°F). Roll out the dough on a floured surface and cut out desired shapes. Place them on flat baking trays and put in freezer or the fridge for at least 20 minutes before baking to preserve shape.

**STEP 6** Bake each tray for 18 minutes, turning halfway to ensure consistency.

**STEP 7** Allow to cool completely before decorating.

# DARK GINGERBREAD

## MAKES AROUND 16

250G UNSALTED BUTTER, SOFTENED

1 EGG

1/2 TSP SALT

1 CUP DARK BROWN SUGAR

1 TSP VANILLA ESSENCE

1 TSP GROUND GINGER

1/4 TSP GROUND NUTMEG

1/2 CUP DUTCH COCOA POWDER (SIFTED), PLUS EXTRA FOR ROLLING OUT

5 CUPS FLOUR

1/2 TSP BAKING POWDER

**STEP 1** Place softened butter and brown sugar in a large bowl and mix until smooth (about four minutes).

**STEP 2** Add in vanilla essence and beat in egg, until combined.

**STEP 3** Sift together spices and Dutch cocoa powder with flour.

**STEP 4** Slowly beat in the baking powder and the flour mixture, one cup at a time. Beat for at least two minutes, until the dough starts to come together. Remove dough from the bowl and knead it on a surface dusted with cocoa powder.

**STEP 5** Wrap the dough in plastic wrap and place in fridge for at least four hours.

**STEP 6** Preheat oven to 180°C (355°F). Roll out the dough on a cocoa-dusted surface and cut out desired shapes. Place them on flat baking trays and put in freezer or the fridge for at least 20 minutes before baking to preserve shape.

**STEP 7** Bake each tray for 18 minutes, turning halfway to ensure consistency.

**STEP 8** Allow to cool completely before decorating.

# DARK CHOCOLATE BROWNIE BASE

## MAKES AROUND 16

**250G UNSALTED BUTTER, SOFTENED**

**1 EGG**

**1/4 TSP SALT**

**1 CUP DARK BROWN SUGAR**

**1 TSP VANILLA ESSENCE**

**1 CUP DUTCH COCOA POWDER (SIFTED), PLUS EXTRA FOR ROLLING OUT**

**5 CUPS FLOUR**

**1/4 TSP BAKING POWDER**

**STEP 1** Place softened butter and dark brown sugar in a large bowl and mix until smooth (about four minutes).

**STEP 2** Add in vanilla essence and beat in egg, until combined.

**STEP 3** Sift together the Dutch cocoa powder with the flour.

**STEP 4** Slowly beat in the flour mixture, one cup at a time. Beat for two minutes, until the dough starts to pull away from the sides. Remove dough from the bowl and knead on a surface dusted with cocoa powder.

**STEP 5** Wrap the dough in plastic wrap and place in fridge for at least four hours.

**STEP 6** Preheat oven to 180°C (355°F). Roll out the dough on a cocoa-dusted surface and cut out desired shapes. Place them on flat baking trays and put in freezer or the fridge for at least 20 minutes before baking to preserve shape.

**STEP 7** Bake each tray for 18 minutes, turning halfway to ensure consistency.

**STEP 8** Allow to cool completely before decorating.

# ROYAL ICING

**MAKES ENOUGH TO COVER 16 COOKIES**

**1/4 CUP MERINGUE POWDER**

**1/2 CUP WATER**

**750G PURE ICING SUGAR, MORE AS REQUIRED**

**LEMON ESSENCE (OPTIONAL)**

*Note: I always sift my icing sugar before I mix up a batch of royal icing. This prevents tiny granules of sugar from clogging the tips. You can also use a food processor to eliminate any lumps.*

**STEP 1** Place meringue powder in a large bowl with water and mix until light and frothy (around 4 minutes).

**STEP 2** Add in lemon essence.

**STEP 3** Add in the pure icing sugar and mix for two minutes until combined. You may need to add slightly more water if the mixture looks too dry. The royal icing should be shiny and smooth but also stiff. You should be able to turn the mixing bowl upside down without it falling out!

**STEP 4** Place plastic wrap over surface of the mixture to ensure it doesn't dry out. Use as required.

# BAKING TIPS AND TRICKS

## A NOTE ABOUT OVENS AND BAKING TIMES

Ovens can be temperamental. One oven's fan-forced 180°C (355°F) can be another oven's 190°C (375°F). The only way to really know what temperature your oven gets to is by using an oven thermometer and testing it. I use a fan-forced oven for all my baking, as the heat distributes evenly and although I follow the 18 minutes average baking time set out in the recipes, I sometimes find that the thickness of my cookies affects how golden they are. So I recommend watching your cookies as they bake, at least the first few times so you get to know how long it takes to reach the desired crispness. I like my cookies slightly caramelised and brown around the edges, but many cookie decorators prefer their 'blank canvasses' to be pale and just cooked so that the icing looks better. But giving them a few extra minutes means there is less chance of them falling apart when the icing goes on; this is important if you're icing bigger surfaces, like the walls and roof of a gingerbread house. Use the baking time as a guide but make your own adjustments to suit your taste and aesthetic.

Always freeze or refrigerate your cookies for at least 20 minutes before you bake them; this relaxes the gluten in the mixture, reduces cookie 'spread' and helps your cookies keep their lovely shape during baking.

## A NOTE ABOUT CUTTERS

Beware that collecting cookie cutters can be utterly addictive and before you know it, you have over 300 of them (all completely necessary, I assure you)! Selecting the right cutter for the job can be as much fun as decorating, but don't forget how size will affect the number of biscuits you get out of one batch of dough. If you look after your cutters, they can last a lifetime and copper ones make lovely family heirlooms. Don't soak them in water; this will erode the metal. A wipe with a warm dishcloth will suffice.

## COOKIE STORAGE

Fresh cookies, kept in an airtight container, are best eaten within 7 days. You can prolong their shelf-life to 3 months by sealing them in cellophane bags with a heat sealer.

Baked, un-iced cookies can be kept frozen for up to 6 months but they must be sealed tightly in a container so no moisture gets in. Thaw and ice as required but don't refreeze them again.

Uncooked cookie dough should be kept in the fridge, sealed in plastic wrap to prevent freezer burn and baked within 5 days. It can be frozen for up to 3 months.

# ICING TIPS AND TRICKS

Using a combination of three different consistencies of royal icing (stiff, piping and flood icing) is crucial to achieving success and simply about how much water you add to the mix. The best way to add water is by using a spritzer bottle so you can control the amount. Use a clean mixing bowl for each kind of icing you make up and always cover the surface with plastic wrap when you're not working with it; it can harden in minutes and can't be resoftened with water. Knowing which icing to use for each project can be a matter of trial and error, but if you know the basics you have a better chance of getting it right the first time. I use a toothpick to spread the icing across the surface of the cookie; some use a dedicated scribing tool, available from decorating shops.

**STIFF ICING** for lettering, fine detail and gluing biscuits together. You shouldn't need to water down the icing too much. You don't want it so stiff it will break your hand, but you do want it to hold its shape. One or two spritzes with the spray bottle should be enough!

**PIPING ICING** for piping outlines. Spritz the icing with water and mix until it's smooth but not too runny. One way to check the consistency is the 'ribbon trick': Dip a spoon into the mix and drizzle a ribbon of icing across the surface. The icing should 'sit' on top of the surface for around 20 seconds before slowly sinking in.

**FLOOD ICING** for filling in shapes. Keep spritzing the icing with water and mixing until it's smooth and very runny. Do your ribbon trick again, but this time, the drizzle should take around 5 seconds or less to sink in.

## A NOTE ABOUT DRYING TIMES

Drying times for the icing will vary but as a general rule:

**STIFF ICING** Takes 5 minutes or less to dry. You need to work quickly with stiff icing as it goes rock hard once it sets.

**PIPING ICING** Takes 20 minutes or less to dry. If you're piping around a shape and adding flooding icing into the middle, use a toothpick to blend the piping and flooding icing together so the outline is less obvious.

**FLOOD ICING** Takes between 8 and 12 hours to dry.

You can use an electric fan to speed up drying time. You can also use a dehydrator – the heat will 'set' the top layer of icing and reduce drying time considerably. Neither is necessary, but worth considering if you want to elevate your icing interest from hobby to professional!

Each coloured section of an iced cookie must be allowed ample time to dry, otherwise you risk the colours bleeding into each other. This means that icing can sometimes take up to 24 or even 48 hours, depending on how much detail you have. While drying, keep your cookie in an airtight container and don't allow anything to touch the surface or you might undo all your hard work.

### A NOTE ABOUT COLOURS

The best dye to use in royal icing is food gel colour. There are quite a few brands and the most popular are stocked in cake decorating shops; you can also order them online. Some are better than others so experiment to see what suits your colour palette best. I don't like to mix more than three colours together, as I find the result can be uneven. I prefer to buy ready-made colours but you can mix your own. American cookie queen Callye Alvarado (AKA Sweet Sugarbelle) hosts some fantastic colour charts on her website www.sweetsugarbelle.com. Check out her blog anyway just to pick up extra icing tips and admire Callye's stunning cookie art!

I recommend tinting royal icing with one toothpick's worth of colour at a time. You can always add more colour, but once you've added too much you can't reverse it. Note that untinted royal icing still needs to be coloured with white food dye as it sets grey, not white!

### A NOTE ABOUT ICING BAGS

Bakers are creatures of habit. Perhaps because we've experienced so many baking and icing disasters (butter bleed is really a thing!), we're superstitious about using other brands or doing things out of order. But the truth about icing bags is that *it really doesn't matter what kind you use.*

I prefer disposable ones, because washing out a reusable bag when you've got eight colours going at the same time makes you madder than a March Hare!

You'll need a coupler for each piping bag; this is a two-piece plastic device which keeps the tip securely in place as you ice. To use, push the large section into the piping bag, cut the tip off the bag, fit your tip onto the nozzle then screw on with the smaller coupler section.

## A NOTE ABOUT ICING TIPS

Icing tips are available from cake decorating stores and online. Buy a few of each as you don't want to be cleaning them out for each colour as you go! Here's a guide to the tips I've used in this book:

**1.5 MM TIP** Best for fine scrollwork, lettering and small details. Sometimes very fine particles can get stuck in this tiny tip, so keep toothpicks on hand for de-clogging.

**2MM TIP** Best for piping outlines and thicker lettering.

**3MM TIP** Best for flooding as the wide tip allows the icing to flow easily.

## TRICKS OF THE TRADE

- Wet-on-wet icing. This technique involves using two flood-consistency colours to achieve a 'flat' look, so the elements sit together on a single surface. Polka dots and paisley swirls work particularly well with this method.

- Uncoloured, royal icing will last 24 hours – it doesn't need to be refrigerated but it does need to be covered with plastic wrap or it will crust over.

- Icing that has been tinted with food dye usually lasts around 4 hours before the mixture starts to separate. After that the colour will be mottled and watery.

- Use sharp toothpicks to spread icing into small spaces and pop any air bubbles. Tapping the cookie gently on a flat surface will bring the bubbles to the surface.

- Rose spirit or cake decorator's essence is a very fast drying alcohol-based liquid that can be used to turn edible lustre dust into paint. The alcohol content evaporates very quickly and doesn't erode the surface of the royal icing the way water does. Use a paint brush to mix a tiny amount of lustre dust with the rose spirit and apply to your cookie.

## A NOTE ABOUT BAKING TOOLS

There are a couple of basic tools you'll need to get started and can be found in any kitchen supplies or specialist baking shops:

- A silicon mat for rolling out cookie dough (I also use a sheet of baking paper between the rolling pin and the dough so it doesn't stick)
- Baking paper for lining cookie sheets/baking trays
- Rolling pin
- Cutters
- Edible ink marker (available in a variety of colours)
- Icing tips
- Icing bags
- Couplers
- Toothpicks

## A NOTE ABOUT DECORATIONS AND INGREDIENTS

Give your imagination free rein and go crazy with cookie decorations! Find these at specialist baking shops:

- Edible dust (or lustre dust)
- Edible paint (pre-made rose spirit mixed with lustre dust)
- Edible shimmer spray (sold in cans)
- Edible gold leaf (use tweezers to apply)
- Rose spirit (turns lustre dust into paint)
- Cachous (small edible pearls)
- Sprinkles
- Stencils
- Culinary lavender (best found in online ingredient stores)

# ACKNOWLEDGEMENTS

This book would not have been possible without a number of special people who championed it from the beginning and helped me eat my way through many delicious biscuit 'failures'.

Thank you to my family for waiting patiently for me to finish taking 'photos' before you devoured the baked goods.

A big thank you to my lovely publisher and editor Roberta Ivers for believing in this project and being available at all hours to talk books and biscuits. Thanks to the Simon & Schuster Australia marketing team for all your hard work, and to the very talented Christa Moffitt for her inspired design.

Many thanks to all the great authors who bravely submit their work for public consumption; please keep writing so we can continue to enjoy visiting other worlds without leaving our bedrooms – or kitchens!

Lastly, thank you to my supportive cookie friends and social media family (you know who you are) for sharing tips, tricks and your love of literature with me. It's been a privilege to share this journey with you.

**LAUREN CHATER** writes fiction with a particular focus on women's stories. After working for many years in a variety of media roles, she turned her passion for reading and research into a professional pursuit. *The Lace Weaver*, her first novel, was published by Simon & Schuster Australia in 2018 and she is currently working on her second, *Gulliver's Wife*, which will be published in 2019. In addition to writing fiction, Lauren established *The Well Read Cookie*, a blog which celebrates her love of baking and literature. She lives in Sydney with her husband and two children.

Find out more at www.laurenchater.com

www.thewellreadcookie.com

www.instagram.com/the_well_read_cookie

www.facebook.com/LaurenChaterWriter

WELL READ COOKIES

First published in Australia in 2018 by

Simon & Schuster (Australia) Pty Limited

Suite 19A, Level 1, Building C, 450 Miller Street, Cammeray, NSW 2062

10 9 8 7 6 5 4 3 2 1

A CBS Company

Sydney New York London Toronto New Delhi

Visit our website at www.simonandschuster.com.au

A catalogue record for this book is available from the National Library of Australia

Designed and typeset by Christabella Designs

Photography by Lauren Chater

Printed by Asia Pacific Offset Ltd

MIX
Paper from responsible sources
FSC® C136333
FSC
www.fsc.org